Where the Money Goes

Understanding Litigant Expenditures for Producing Electronic Discovery

Nicholas M. Pace, Laura Zakaras

RAND Institute for Civil Justice

A RAND LAW, BUSINESS, AND REGULATION INSTITUTE

This research was conducted by the RAND Institute for Civil Justice, a research institute within RAND Law, Business, and Regulation, a division of the RAND Corporation.

Library of Congress Cataloging-in-Publication Data

Pace, Nicholas M. (Nicholas Michael), 1955-
Where the money goes : understanding litigant expenditures for producing electronic discovery / Nicholas M. Pace, Laura Zakaras.
p. cm.
Includes bibliographical references.
ISBN 978-0-8330-6876-7 (pbk. : alk. paper)
1. Electronic discovery (Law) I. Zakaras, Laura. II. Title.-

K2247.P33 2012
347.73'57—dc23

2012011130

The RAND Corporation is a nonprofit institution that helps improve policy and decisionmaking through research and analysis. RAND's publications do not necessarily reflect the opinions of its research clients and sponsors.

Published 2012 by the RAND Corporation
1776 Main Street, P.O. Box 2138, Santa Monica, CA 90407-2138
1200 South Hayes Street, Arlington, VA 22202-5050
4570 Fifth Avenue, Suite 600, Pittsburgh, PA 15213-2665
RAND URL: http://www.rand.org/
To order RAND documents or to obtain additional information, contact
Distribution Services: Telephone: (310) 451-7002;
Fax: (310) 451-6915; Email: order@rand.org

Preface

This monograph addresses one of the most persistent challenges of conducting litigation in the era of digital information: the costs of complying with discovery requests, particularly the costs of review. Using case studies of eight large corporations and a review of the literature on electronic discovery (e-discovery), we estimate the dimensions of those costs and identify effective ways to reduce them. We also examine the challenges of preserving electronic information and recommend steps that can be taken to address them.

This research was conducted by the RAND Institute for Civil Justice (ICJ), a research institute within RAND Law, Business, and Regulation (LBR). The ICJ is dedicated to improving the civil justice system by supplying policymakers and the public with rigorous and independent research. Its studies analyze litigation trends and outcomes, evaluate policy options, and bring together representatives of different interests to debate alternative solutions to policy problems. The ICJ builds on a long tradition of RAND research characterized by an interdisciplinary, empirical approach to public policy issues and rigorous standards of quality, objectivity, and independence.

LBR, a research division of the RAND Corporation, is dedicated to improving policy and decisionmaking in civil justice, corporate ethics and governance, and business regulation. It serves policymakers and executives in both government and the private sector through research and analysis on controversial and challenging issues in these areas.

Research is supported by pooled grants from a range of sources, including corporations, trade and professional associations, individuals, government agencies, and private foundations. It disseminates its work widely to policymakers, practitioners in law and business, other researchers, and the public. In accordance with RAND policy, all its reports are subject to peer review. Its publications do not necessarily reflect the opinions or policies of its research sponsors.

For more information on LBR, see http://lbr.rand.org or contact the director:

James Dertouzos
Director, RAND Law, Business, and Regulation
1776 Main Street
P.O. Box 2138
Santa Monica, CA 90407-2138
310-393-0411 x7476
James_Dertouzos@rand.org

For more information on the ICJ, see http://lbr.rand.org/icj or contact the research director:

Paul Heaton
Director for Research, RAND Institute for Civil Justice
1776 Main Street
P.O. Box 2138
Santa Monica, CA 90407-2138
310-393-0411 x7526
Paul_Heaton@rand.org

Contents

Figures

Tables

Summary

Pretrial discovery procedures are designed to encourage an exchange of information that will help narrow the issues being litigated, eliminate surprise at trial, and achieve substantial justice. But, in recent years, claims have been made that the societal shift from paper documents to electronically stored information (ESI) has led to sharper increases in discovery costs than in the overall cost of litigation.

In response, the Federal Rules of Civil Procedure have been amended several times in the past five years, and most states have adopted or amended rules of procedure or evidence to address a range of challenges posed by e-discovery. This evolution in the rules is ongoing: The federal Advisory Committee on Civil Rules is currently exploring issues related to the costs of discovery and may well be on track to propose further amendments to the federal civil rules. Few other issues about the civil justice system in recent years have so focused the attention of policymakers and stakeholders.

Study Purpose and Approach

We hope this monograph will help inform the debate by addressing the following research questions:

- What are the costs associated with different phases of e-discovery production?
- How are these costs distributed across internal and external sources of labor, resources, and services?
- How can these costs be reduced without compromising the quality of the discovery process?
- What do litigants perceive to be the key challenges of preserving electronic information?

We chose a case-study method that identified eight very large companies that were willing, with our assurances of confidentiality, to provide in-depth information about e-discovery production expenses. The companies consisted of one each from the communications, electronics, energy, household care products, and insurance fields, and three from the pharmaceutical/biotechnology/medical device field. We asked participants to choose a minimum of five cases in which they produced data and electronic documents to another party as part of an e-discovery request. In the end, we received at least some reliable e-discovery production cost data for 57 cases, including traditional lawsuits and regulatory investigations.

We also collected information from extensive interviews with key legal personnel from these companies. Our interviews focused on how each company responds to new requests for e-discovery, what steps it takes in anticipation of those requests, the nature and size of the company's information technology (IT) infrastructure, its document-retention policies and disaster-recovery and archiving practices, its litigation pressure and the types of cases in which it is involved, and what it finds to be the key challenges in this evolving e-discovery environment.

Our analysis is also informed by an extensive review of the legal and technical literature on e-discovery, with emphasis on the intersection of information-retrieval science and the law. We supplemented our data collection with additional interviews with representatives of participating companies, focusing on issues related to the preservation of information in anticipation of discovery demands in current or potential litigation.

Because the participating companies and cases do not constitute a representative sample of corporations and litigation, we cannot draw generalizations from our findings that apply to all corporate litigants or all discovery productions. However, the case-study approach provides a richly detailed account of the resources required by a diverse set of very large companies operating in different industries to comply with what they described as typical e-discovery requests. In what follows, we highlight our key findings.

Costs of Producing Electronic Documents

We organized the cost data we received into three tasks:

- *Collection* consists of locating potential sources of ESI following the receipt of a demand to produce electronic documents and data, and gathering ESI for further use in the e-discovery process, such as processing or review.
- *Processing* is reducing the volume of collected ESI through automated processing techniques, modifying it if necessary to forms more suitable for review, analysis, and other tasks.
- *Review* is evaluating digital information to identify relevant and responsive documents to produce, and privileged documents or confidential or sensitive information to withhold.

There were, of course, some gaps in the data. But the data were sufficiently complete to provide interesting insights about relative costs and level of effort across tasks. Figure S.1, for example, shows that the major cost component in our cases was the review of documents for relevance, responsiveness, and privilege (typically about 73 percent). Collection, an area on which policymakers have focused intensely in the past, consumed about 8 percent of expenditures for the cases in our study, while processing costs consumed about 19 percent in typical cases.

We also examined the costs of collection, processing, and review in terms of their sources: *internal*, such as law department counsel and IT department staff; *vendors*; and *outside counsel*. As might be expected because of their historical role in the review process, expenditures for the services of outside counsel consumed about 70 percent of total e-discovery production costs. Internal expenditures, even with adjustments made for underreporting, were generally around 4 percent of the total, while vendor expenditures were around 26 percent (Figure S.1). As Table S.1 shows, vendors played the dominant role in collection and processing, while review was largely the domain of outside counsel. The zero counts for internal processing and review do not mean that corporate resources were not consumed for these tasks, only that none of the

Figure S.1
Relative Costs of Producing Electronic Documents

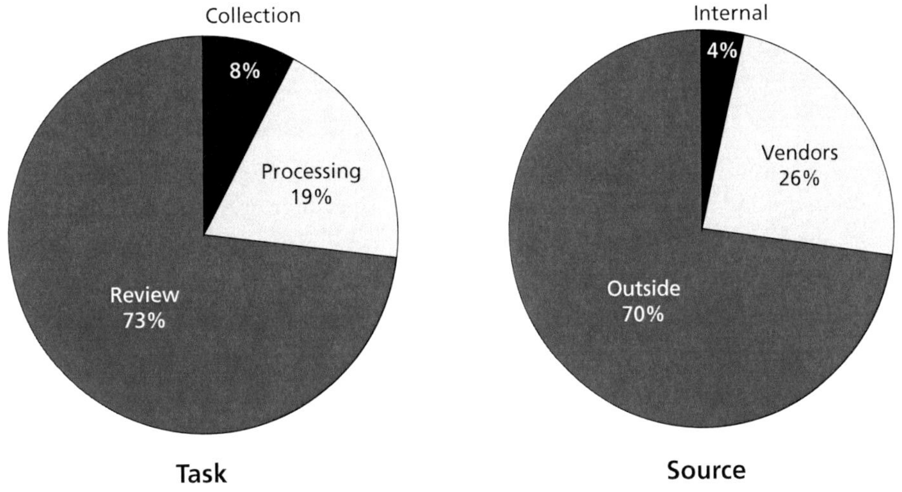

NOTE: Values reflect median percentages for cases with complete data, adjusted to 100 percent.
RAND *MG1208-S.1*

Table S.1
Case Counts by the Primary Source of Expenditures for E-Discovery Tasks

Task	Internal	Vendor	Outside Counsel	Total Cases Reporting
Collection	6	31	5	42
Processing	0	42	2	44
Review	0	4	45	49

cases reporting complete information had internal expenditures for such activities that were greater than those for external entities, such as vendors or outside counsel.

The task breakdown in the table, however, appears likely to change in the future. Most of the companies whose representatives we interviewed expressed a commitment to taking on more e-discovery tasks themselves and outsourcing those that could be "commoditized." Collection is a good example of this trend. Two of the eight companies were in the process of implementing an automated, cross-network collection tool in order to perform such services without the need for outside vendors, and others were anticipating moving in that direction. Although we found little evidence that the review process was moving in-house, the legal departments in the companies from which we interviewed representatives were taking greater control over at least the "first-pass" review to confirm relevance and responsiveness of documents, choosing vendors and specialized legal service law firms to perform such functions that were formerly delegated to outside counsel.

Reducing the Cost of Review

With more than half of our cases reporting that review consumed at least 70 percent of the total costs of document production, this single area is an obvious target for reducing e-discovery expenditures. We believe that many stakeholder complaints would diminish if expenditures for review were no more burdensome than those for either the collection or processing phase. Because review consumes about $0.73 of every dollar spent on ESI production, while collection and processing consume about $0.08 and $0.19, respectively, *review costs would have to be reduced by about three-quarters* in order to make those costs comparable to processing, the next most costly component of production. Choosing a 75-percent reduction in review expenditures as the desired target is an admittedly arbitrary decision, but more-modest cost savings are not likely to end criticisms from some quarters that the advent of e-discovery has caused an unacceptable increase in the costs of resolving large-scale disputes. To explore possible ways of achieving this target, we synthesized the methods that research on this topic has identified as promising for cutting review costs, both for the traditional approach of an "eyes-on" review of each document and for moving to a new paradigm that relies on computer-categorized review technology to examine documents for relevance, responsiveness, or privilege. We also summarize the literature on the relative quality of traditional review practices and computerized approaches to assess whether moving away from human review would compromise the quality of the process.

Significant Reduction in Current Labor Costs Is Unlikely

Companies are trying a variety of alternatives to the traditional use of outside law firms for most review tasks. In order to reduce the cost of review-related labor, they may hire temporary attorneys or use legal process outsourcing (LPO) companies with stables of contract attorneys. However, the rates currently paid to such project attorneys during large-scale reviews in the United States may well have bottomed out, with further reductions of any significant size unlikely. Another option that has been explored is the use of English-speaking local lawyers in such countries as India and the Philippines. Although such foreign outsourcing uses local attorneys who will work for much less than U.S. counsel, issues related to information security, oversight, maintaining attorney-client privilege, and logistics may limit the utility of offshore approaches for most litigation.

Increasing the Rate of Review Has Its Limits

The most-expansive claims regarding review speed is about 100 documents per hour, and this number assumes that reviewers have the strongest motivations and experience and are examining documents simple enough that a decision on relevance, responsiveness, privilege, or confidential information could be made in an average of 36 seconds. A trained "speed reader" can skim written materials at roughly 1,000 words per minute with about 50-percent comprehension. Therefore, even allocating zero time for bringing up a new document on the screen and zero time for contemplating a decision or the act of clicking the appropriate button to indicate a choice, a maximum of 600 words (about a page and a half) can be read in 36 seconds. Given the trade-off between reading speed and comprehension, especially in light of the complexity of documents subject to discovery in large-scale litigation, it is unrealistic to expect much room for improvement in the rates of unassisted human review.

Techniques for Grouping Documents Are Not the Answer

We describe three techniques that are increasingly used to organize documents—and, in some cases, "bulk-code" like documents—to streamline the review process:

- *Near-duplicate detection* groups together documents that contain mostly identical blocks of text or other information but that nevertheless differ in some minor way (any truly duplicate documents should have been removed during the processing phase).
- *Clustering* identifies the keywords and concepts in each document then groups documents by the degree to which they share keywords or concepts so that documents can be organized by topic rather than in random order to streamline the review.
- *Email threading* groups individual emails into single "conversations," sorting chronologically, and eliminating duplicate material.

These techniques organize material rather than reducing the number of documents in the review set. Commercial vendors of these services claim they can increase the rate of review to 200, 300, or even 500 documents per hour. However, given the physical limitations of reading and comprehension, better organization of the corpus of documents is not likely to account for such astonishing review rates unless decisions about individual documents can be applied to dozens or hundreds of similar items on a routine basis. Although some document sets may lend themselves to bulk coding in this manner, it is unlikely that these techniques would foster sufficiently dramatic improvements in review speed for most large-scale reviews.

Human Reviewers Are Highly Inconsistent

Just how accurate is the traditional approach in these days of computerized review tools flashing documents on screen before a first-year associate or contract lawyer at rates exceeding 50 documents per hour? Some rigorous studies addressing this issue found that human reviewers often disagree with one another when they review the same set of documents for relevance and responsiveness in large-scale reviews. In one study, for example, seven teams of attorneys, all trained in a similar manner and given the same instructions, examined 28,000 documents, clustered into 12,000 families involving similar topics, to judge whether the families were responsive to the facts of the case.[1] The seven teams differed significantly on the percentage of families determined to be responsive, ranging from a low of 23 percent to a high of 54 percent. As indicated by other studies discussed in this monograph, the high level of disagreement, corroborated by other studies discussed in the main text, is caused by human error in applying the criteria for inclusion, not a lack of clarity in the document's meaning or ambiguity in how the scope of the production demand should be interpreted.

Is Predictive Coding an Answer?

We believe that one way to achieve substantial savings in producing massive amounts of electronic information would be to let computers do the heavy lifting for review. Predictive coding is a type of computer-categorized review application that classifies documents according to how well they match the concepts and terms in sample documents. Such machine-learning techniques continually refine the computer's classifications with input from users, just as spam filters self-correct to increase the reliability of their future decisions about new email mes-

---

[1] Barnett and Godjevac, 2011.

sages, until the ambiguous ratings disappear. With predictive coding, humans (i.e., attorneys) initially examine samples of documents from the review set and make determinations about whether they are relevant, responsive, or privileged. Using those decisions, the software assigns scores to each document in the review set representing the probability that a document matches the desired characteristics. Additional samples of these new decisions are drawn and examined by the attorney reviewers, and the application refines the templates it uses to assign scores. The results of this iterative process are eventually stabilized. At that point, disagreement between the software's decisions and those of human reviewers should be minimized.

Because this is nascent technology, there is little research on how the accuracy of predictive coding compares with that of human review. The few studies that exist, however, generally suggest that predictive coding identifies at least as many documents of interest as traditional eyes-on review with about the same level of inconsistency, and there is some evidence to suggest that it can do better than that.

Not surprisingly, costs of predictive coding, even with the use of relatively experienced counsel for machine-learning tasks, are likely to be substantially lower than the costs of human review. It should be kept in mind that attorney review is still very much in play with predictive coding, but generally only for the smaller subset of documents that the application has judged to be potentially relevant, responsive, or privileged.[2] Because there is scant research on the issue, it is too early to confidently estimate the magnitude of any savings. Evidence, however, suggests the reduction in person-hours required to review a large-scale document production could be considerable. One study, for example, which did not report on cost savings but did report time savings, suggested that predictive coding of a document set previously reviewed in the traditional way would have saved about 80 percent in attorney review hours.[3] Although this estimate did not include the costs of the vendor's services, and the potential reduction in hours would be strongly influenced by the threshold probability scores used for determining potential matches, the savings are still likely to be considerable and meet the goal we set of a three-quarter reduction in review expenditures.

Barriers to the Use of Computer-Categorized Document Review

With such potential to reduce the costs of review without compromising quality, why is it that predictive coding and other computer-categorized document review techniques are not being embraced by litigants? None of the companies in our sample was using predictive coding for review purposes; at the end of 2011, we could find no evidence in the published record that any vendor, law firm, or litigant had used predictive coding in a publicized case that named the parties and court jurisdiction.

Some concerns are likely to pose barriers to the use of predictive coding, including whether it performs well in any of the following:

- identifying *all* potentially responsive documents while avoiding *any* overproduction

---

[2] For example, one potential approach to computer-categorized document review would have the application identify documents likely to be relevant and responsive and then have attorneys examine only the identified set to confirm the decisions and to determine whether those documents contain privileged communications or sensitive information.

[3] Equivio, 2009a.

- identifying privileged or confidential information
- flagging "smoking guns" and other crucial documents
- classifying highly technical documents
- reviewing relatively small document sets.

Another barrier to widespread use could well be resistance to the idea from outside counsel, who would stand to lose a historical revenue stream. Outside counsel may also be reluctant to expose their clients to the risks of adopting an evolving technology. But perhaps most important is the absence of judicial guidance on the matter. At the time we conducted this study, there were simply no judicial decisions that squarely approved or disapproved of the use of predictive coding or similar computer-categorized techniques for review purposes. It is also true that many attorneys would be uncomfortable with the idea of being an early adopter when the potential downside risks appear to be so large. Few lawyers would want to be placed in the uncomfortable position of having to argue that a predictive-coding strategy reflects reasonable precautions taken to prevent inadvertent disclosure, overproduction, or underproduction, especially when no one else seems to be using it.

We propose that the best way to overcome these barriers and bring predictive coding into the mainstream is for innovative, public-spirited litigants to take bold steps by using this technology for large-scale e-discovery efforts and to proclaim its use in an open and transparent manner. The motivation for conducting successful public demonstrations of this promising technology would be to win judicial approvals in a variety of jurisdictions, which, in turn, could lead to the routine use of various computer-categorized techniques in large-scale reviews along with long-term cost savings for the civil justice system as a whole. Without organizational litigants making a contribution in this manner, many millions of dollars in litigation expenditures will be wasted each year until legal tradition catches up with modern technology.

Challenges of Preservation

Some important generalizations emerged from our inquiry into what corporate counsel consider to be the main challenges of preserving electronic information in anticipation of litigation.

Companies Are Not Tracking the Costs of Preservation

Most interviewees did not hesitate to confess that their preservation costs had not been systematically tracked in any way and that they were unclear as to how such tracking might be accomplished, though collecting useful metrics was generally asserted as an important future goal for the company.

Preservation Expenditures Are Said to Be Significant

All interviewees reported that preservation had evolved into a significant portion of their companies' total e-discovery expenditures. Some of them believed that preserving information was now costing them more than producing e-discovery in the aggregate. The way in which organizations perceive the size of preservation expenditures relative to that of production appears to be related to steps taken (or not taken) to move away from ad hoc preservation strategies, the nature of their caseloads, and ongoing impacts on computing services and business practices.

There Are Complaints About the Absence of Clear Legal Authority

A key concern voiced by the interviewees was their uncertainty about what strategies are defensible ones for preservation duties. Determining the reasonable scope for a legal hold in terms of custodians, data locations, and volume was said to be a murky process at best, with strong incentives to overpreserve in the face of the risk for significant sanctions. Similar concerns were voiced about the process itself, with few concrete guideposts said to be available to provide litigants with a level of comfort when deciding not only what to preserve, but how.

The cause for such worries is the absence of controlling legal authority in this area. Although judicial decisions have addressed preservation scope and process, they act as legally binding precedent in only specific jurisdictions, or conflict with decisions rendered by other courts on the same issues. As a result, litigants reported that they were greatly concerned about not making defensible decisions involving preservation and about the looming potential of serious sanctions.

Recommendations

We propose three recommendations to address the complaints of excessive costs and uncertainty that emerged from our interviews.

Adopt Computer Categorization to Reduce the Costs of Review in Large-Scale E-Discovery Efforts

The increasing volume of digital records makes predictive coding and other computer-categorized review techniques not only a cost-effective option to help conduct review but the *only* reasonable way to handle large-scale production. Despite efforts to cull data as much as possible during processing, review sets in some cases may be impossible to examine thoroughly using humans, at least not in time frames that make sense during ongoing litigation. New court rules *might* move the process forward, but the best catalyst for more-widespread use of predictive coding would be well-publicized documentation of cases in which judges examined the results of actual computer-categorized reviews. It will be up to forward-thinking litigants to make that happen.

It should be noted that we believe that computer-categorized review techniques, such as predictive coding, have their greatest utility with production volumes that are at least as large as the cases in our sample.

Improve Tracking of Costs of Production and Preservation

There are many reasons to track discovery costs. Without such data, companies cannot develop strategies for dealing with massive data volumes, such as investing in automated legal-hold–compliance systems or advanced analytic software for early case assessment. A litigant also needs to be able to present a credible argument to a judge that a proposed discovery plan or request will result in unreasonably large expenditures. Finally, the need for better records may be strongest in the context of preservation, in which the absence of publicly reported data in this area frustrates rule-making efforts intended to address litigant complaints.

Bring Certainty to Legal Authority Concerning Preservation

Steps must be taken soon to address litigant concerns about complying with preservation duties. The absence of clear, unambiguous, and transjurisdictional legal authority is thwarting thoughtful preservation efforts, potentially leading to overpreservation at considerable cost; and creating uncertainty about proper scope, defensible processes, and sanctionable behavior.

Acknowledgments

Our sincerest thanks go to the attorneys, paralegals, and IT staff at the companies participating in the data collection. They were always generous with their time and patiently responded to numerous requests for follow-up contact. We greatly appreciate their frank and thoughtful insights into the challenges litigants face in responding to e-discovery demands and preserving data in anticipation of such requests. Their employers are also to be commended for appreciating the need for empirical research in this area. Their willingness to share sensitive information with project staff and allow us access to personnel and records is a reflection of the importance of the policy debate regarding e-discovery.

Throughout the course of this work, we consulted with Thomas Y. Allman, an attorney, consultant, and authority in the area of the management of electronically stored information and corporate compliance. His unselfish assistance in helping us understand numerous aspects of e-discovery law and public policy was invaluable.

Lisa Bernard performed her usual professional and thorough job of editing and organizing the final version of the monograph. Christopher Dirks, Stephanie Tjioe, Joan Myers, Stacie McKee, Michelle Platt, and Pamela Calig all did wonderful jobs in addressing the administrative aspects of this study. Robert H. Anderson and James N. Dertouzos were instrumental in the background research, study design, and data-collection phases of this project.

Jason R. Baron, James M. Anderson, Siddhartha Dalal, and an anonymous external reviewer provided helpful criticisms and contributions in their formal reviews of this monograph. We value their suggestions and hope that we have responded appropriately.

We are also grateful for the input of various members of the ICJ Board of Overseers who took the time to review early drafts of this monograph. Their comments gave the authors an invaluable education and grounded the end result in reality.

Any errors in methodology, data collection, or conclusions are, of course, solely our responsibility.

Abbreviations

ABA	American Bar Association
BLS	Bureau of Labor Statistics
DESI	Discovery of Electronically Stored Information
EDRM	Electronic Discovery Reference Model
ESI	electronically stored information
FJC	Federal Judicial Center
FRCP	Federal Rules of Civil Procedure
FRE	Federal Rules of Evidence
GB	gigabyte
ICAIL	International Conference on Artificial Intelligence and Law
ICJ	RAND Institute for Civil Justice
IT	information technology
LBR	RAND Law, Business, and Regulation
LPO	legal process outsourcing
NAICS	North American Industry Classification System
NIST	National Institute of Standards and Technology
NPV	negative predictive value
OCR	optical character recognition
PPV	positive predictive value
ROC	receiver operating characteristic
TREC	Text REtrieval Conference

CHAPTER ONE

Introduction

Background

The process by which a party in a civil lawsuit can demand that an opponent produce documents, answer written questions under oath, give sworn testimony, and even submit to a medical examination is one of the defining features of the U.S. civil justice system. Such pretrial discovery procedures, often conducted with little supervision from the judge overseeing the litigation, are designed to help narrow the issues, eliminate surprise at trial, and achieve substantial justice. But, although various issues related to the discovery process have been long been the subject of discussion and debate by lawyers, judges, policymakers, and academics, the most-vocal criticism now seems to have focused on one specific area: costs.

In recent years, some critics have claimed that discovery-related expenditures are so far out of control that they are preventing parties from litigating legitimate disputes.[1] Moreover, claims have been made that the costs associated with discovery constitute "a significant litigation expense, and are likely partially responsible for the disproportionately large amount of litigation spending associated with the U.S. legal system."[2] Although not all of those participating in the civil justice arena call for wholesale discovery reform, there does seem to be general consensus that discovery has become unnecessarily expensive.[3] And, according to some observers, the problem with discovery costs is not a static one, with expenditures said to be ever-increasing in size, with the upward trend variously described as "skyrocketing," "exploding," "runaway," and "spiraling."[4]

What has triggered these claims of exponential growth in the costs of conducting pretrial discovery? The answer is likely to be found in the brave new world of identifying, preserving, examining, processing, and exchanging documents and other information maintained digitally instead of in the traditional paper form. Demands for data and documents in electronic form are now the prime suspect in what is characterized as a disproportional increase in discovery costs compared with the overall expense of litigation.[5] As a result, issues related to what

[1] Driver, 2010b, p. 1, interviewing John H. Martin.

[2] Lawyers for Civil Justice, Civil Justice Reform Group, and U.S. Chamber Institute for Legal Reform, 2010, p. 15.

[3] Though a recent survey of attorneys in the American Bar Association (ABA) Section of Litigation reported that only a slight majority of respondents disagreed with the statement that "current discovery mechanisms work well," 82 percent of the respondents agreed that discovery was too expensive (ABA, 2009b, Tables 6.1 and 11.5).

[4] Lawyers for Civil Justice, 2010, p. 2; Sharpe, 2009, p. 115; Schulman and Birnbaum, 2010, p. 24; Wells, 2008.

[5] ABA, 2009b, Table 7.4. Three-quarters of respondents in that survey agreed with the statement, "Discovery costs, as a share of total litigation costs, have increased disproportionately due to the advent of e-discovery."

has become known as electronic discovery (e-discovery) of electronically stored information (ESI) have "renewed and amplified" discussions of whether federal and state court rules, procedures, and judicial guidance surrounding the pretrial discovery process are in any need of revision.[6] To deal with the many challenges posed by electronic discovery, rule-makers extensively amended existing Rules 26 and 34 of the Federal Rules of Civil Procedure (FRCP) in 2006; a new Rule 502 of the Federal Rules of Evidence (FRE) was enacted in 2008;[7] and, by early 2011, 37 states had adopted or amended rules of procedure or evidence that addressed various issues related to e-discovery.[8] And the evolution in the rules does not appear to be over: At the request of the Judicial Conference of the United States' Standing Committee on Rules of Practice and Procedure, the Advisory Committee on Civil Rules sponsored a conference at Duke University School of Law in May 2010 to "explore the current costs of civil litigation, particularly discovery, and to discuss possible solutions."[9] As a result of the Duke Conference, as well as follow-on work, the advisory committee may well be on track to propose additional amendments to the federal civil rules.[10] Few other issues in the civil justice arena in recent years have so completely captured the attention of policymakers and stakeholders.[11]

Although the most–widely circulated critiques of the current state of e-discovery seem to originate with advocacy groups representing corporate interests or attorneys with predominantly defense or corporate (*in-house*) counsel practices, similar concerns have been voiced by some lawyers who primarily represent plaintiffs. Some recent attorney surveys suggest that at least a portion of the plaintiffs' bar also perceives e-discovery as a factor driving the cost of resolving disputes. For example, a survey of members of an organization made up primarily of attorneys representing workers in labor, employment, and civil rights disputes reported that 61 percent of respondents agreed with the statement that e-discovery increases the costs of litigation.[12] And noted plaintiffs' attorneys have acknowledged that, because "ESI is different

---

[6] According to the Judicial Conference of the United States, 2010b, p. 1,

> [T]he litigation landscape has changed with astonishing rapidity, largely reflecting the revolution in information technology. The advent and wide use of electronic discovery renewed and amplified the complaints that the existing rules and practices are inadequate to achieve the promise of Rule 1: a just, speedy, and inexpensive resolution to every civil action in the federal courts.

[7] FRCP 26 describes a litigant's duty to make an early disclosure of various types of information and sets forth general provisions about discovery. FRCP 34 controls discovery related to the production of documents, electronically stored information, and other tangible things. FRE 502 addresses issues related to the attorney-client privilege and work-product protection.

[8] See Allman, 2011a, p. 1.

[9] Judicial Conference of the United States, 2010a.

[10] Allman, 2011b.

[11] Intuitively, the move from paper-based recordkeeping to more-efficient electronic processes presumably should have reduced the costs of pretrial information exchange. Although this may hold true for document productions of modest size (and certainly the expenses associated with a delivery of a single data CD will be far less than those for a delivery of thousands of bankers' boxes filled with an equivalent volume of information in paper documents), the financial impact of discovery on producing parties is said to have increased

> because the sheer volume of records that are identifiable and producible is greater with electronic processes, potentially relevant information that might never have been recorded previously is now being routinely retained, and because the requesting attorneys are aggressive in seeking out such information. (Dertouzos, Pace, and Anderson, 2008, pp. 2–3)

[12] Hamburg, Koski, and Tobias, 2010, p. 36.

in nature from paper-based documents, e-discovery does raise new concerns and problems for which solutions need to be found."[13]

It is against this background that the RAND Institute for Civil Justice (ICJ) initiated a study to examine the costs that are at the heart of much of the criticism in recent years, specifically those for producing information primarily stored in electronic form in response to requests under federal and state discovery rules. The ICJ has a lengthy history of conducting empirical studies of civil litigation, with special emphasis on describing the expenses associated with the pretrial process.[14] In addition, issues surrounding the development of e-discovery have been an integral part of the recent ICJ research agenda, so it made sense to take another look at litigation costs but, in this instance, concentrate on those related to requests for ESI production.[15]

Goals of the Research

This research addresses several research questions:

- What are the costs associated with different phases of e-discovery production?
- How are these costs distributed across internal and external sources of labor, resources, and services?
- How can these costs be reduced without compromising the quality of the discovery process?
- What do litigants perceive to be the key challenges of preserving electronic information?

Approach

Challenges of Conducting Empirical Research on Electronic Discovery

Although every empirical data-collection effort that examines the costs of the civil justice system faces unique challenges, research on pretrial processes, such as discovery, are especially problematic.[16] A repeated lament in the academic and legal literature is that "there has been little or no research into the costs imposed on the larger judicial system by the discovery process," other than studies focusing on the impact on costs wrought by certain discovery-rule changes or arising out of research conducted many decades ago.[17] There has been some recent

[13] Milberg LLC and Hausfeld LLC, 2010, p. 11.

[14] See, e.g., Kakalik, Hensler, et al., 1998; and Kakalik, Dunworth, et al., 1996.

[15] See, e.g., Dertouzos, Pace, and Anderson, 2008.

[16] See, e.g., Hensler, 1995 (discussing the fact that most information about costs is in the hands of private parties); Kritzer, 1983 (discussing the lack of institutional memory among organizational litigants); and McKenna and Wiggins, 1998, pp. 797–799 (discussing the challenges faced in studies of the pretrial process).

[17] Kessler and Rubinfeld, 2007, p. 380. Examples of studies that were able to obtain case-level data on the costs of discovery include Willging, Stienstra, and Shapard, 1998; and Kakalik, Hensler, et al., 1998. In addition, information about discovery expenditures was reported in early studies, such as Trubek et al., 1983, pp. 90–91; and Glaser, 1968, pp. 162–188.

scholarship in response to renewed clamors for discovery reform; however, for the most part, the "actual costs of discovery have rarely been quantified in empirical studies."[18]

The reasons for the scarcity of research on this subject are many:

- *Information about pretrial expenditures is almost always in the exclusive control of litigants and their attorneys.* Outside of very narrow circumstances, parties in the United States are under no obligation to publicly report the amounts they have spent in preparation for trial or in relation to the discovery process.
- *Researchers must collect data from multiple sources*—not just outside counsel, who have traditionally handled the bulk of the pretrial discovery process. Organizational litigants are increasingly taking greater direct control over aspects of the discovery process, and detailed information about those activities and their associated costs may be unknown to outside attorneys.
- *Although closed cases are the most-promising candidates for collecting data on costs, information about them can be difficult to locate.* Memories can fade, files may have been sent to deep storage or culled of all but summary information, or the staff most closely associated with the case may have retired or left for positions elsewhere. It may not always be possible to accurately reconstruct what took place during litigation completed months or years previously.
- *It may be time-consuming or costly for litigants and their attorneys to retrieve relevant data about discovery-related costs.* Unless the information is easily and inexpensively available, there is a good chance that litigants and their attorneys will decline an outsider's request to provide cost data.
- *Staff in corporate departments, such as those in legal and information technology (IT), are unlikely to track their own litigation-related time expenditures.* Data regarding such activities as those associated with a specific discovery production are even less likely to be tracked.
- *Most importantly, organizations may be reluctant to share information about their legal expenditures.* Even when pressured to do so by regulators, "companies are often skittish about disclosing lawsuit costs."[19] Disclosure of information about a lawsuit, including costs incurred, is felt by some corporate defendants and their counsel to run the risk of permitting "plaintiffs to learn or reverse engineer defendants' litigation assessments and strategies."[20] Attorney bills, for example, have been characterized as potentially revealing "the motive of the client in seeking representation, litigation strategy, privileged communications or the specific nature of the services provided by attorneys, such as research into particular areas of the law. . . ."[21]

---

[18] McKenna and Wiggins, 1998, p. 796. See also Lee and Willging, 2009.

[19] Kolker, 2011.

[20] Harrington et al., 2008, p. 11. Even information about fee arrangements has been asserted as potentially revealing litigation strategy and tactics; see, e.g., Shaikin, 2005.

[21] *In Re Grand Jury Witness (Salas, Waxman)*, 695 F.2d 359 at 362 (9th Cir. 1982).

Case-Study Methodology

In light of these challenges, we decided to address our research needs primarily through a case-study methodology. Given the perceived sensitivity of the data and the complexity of the information sought, a large-scale distribution of questionnaires was not likely to yield useful information about litigation-related expenditures in actual cases. Instead, a case-study approach would allow us to reach out directly to potential participants and adequately address their concerns about how the data would be collected, safeguarded, and utilized. Our plan was to persuade a group of companies to provide extensive background on their e-discovery approaches and the challenges they have faced, with a focus on their recent experiences producing electronic documents.

To supplement the case studies, we conducted an extensive literature review of the legal press, law review articles, academic studies, and case law related to e-discovery in the United States, with an emphasis on expenditure information, technical issues, history, organizational responses, and likely trends. Much of that review informed our discussion of the current costs of examining documents for relevance, responsiveness, and privilege, as well as the potential for new technologies to offer cost savings in document reviews (Chapters Four, Five, and Six).

Finally, we conducted interviews with company representatives who were part of our original case studies to assess whether their companies track the costs of preservation, learn how those costs are believed to compare with those associated with production, and better understand what concerns companies have about their responsibility to preserve information for potential litigation, not just for the cases in our study sample but for matters that may never be the subject of a complaint or reach the discovery stage.

In the next section, we describe how we selected the corporations for our study and the lawsuits for our data collection, how we organized our data collection by category and source, and how we conducted our analysis of data preservation.

Selection of Companies and Cases

In identifying potential companies for our study, our primary requirements were that the participants be large corporations with a history of recent litigation and that they be willing to cooperate in the data collection. We sought relatively large entities because we wanted to work with organizations that were addressing e-discovery issues on a regular basis, whose resources permitted a measured and thoughtful response to production demands, and whose corporate staff would have the time available to work closely with us in the data-collection process.

This type of purposive sampling technique relies on the researcher's judgment to select the individual units of the population to be studied; in this particular exercise, our interest was in how organizations with significant assets and litigation exposures have responded to the challenges of e-discovery production. Because we do not use a random sample, we make no claim that the experiences of the companies included in the data collection are generalizable to all large corporations, let alone all corporate litigants.

To locate a set of companies that met these criteria, we drew on contacts we had developed during previous ICJ research in the "e-discovery community,"[22] the loose network of attorneys, vendors, judges, corporate legal department staff, IT professionals, and academics who regularly participate in e-discovery-related conferences and seminars, the Sedona Confer-

[22] Dertouzos, Pace, and Anderson, 2008.

ence's working groups related to e-discovery and information management (IM), and public comment opportunities offered by policymaking bodies considering procedural rule changes. We reached out to various members of that network for suggestions of companies that might be interested in providing in-depth information about e-discovery production expenses. Following up with suggested leads, we contacted companies in a variety of industries, with the hoped-for goal of finding ten participating companies to produce about 60 example cases (given a targeted average of six cases per corporation).

We focused our efforts on corporations that were likely to have been litigants in cases or other legal processes in which they had produced ESI, contacted a member of the legal department in each identified company, explained the nature of our work and the need for detailed cost data, and requested the company's participation in the confidential data collection. As is not uncommon in such research efforts, most of these attempts were unsuccessful, but we eventually located eight companies willing to participate. They consisted of one each from the communications, electronics, energy, household care products, and insurance fields and three from the pharmaceutical/biotechnology/medical device field. All but one of these companies had annual revenues that would have made them eligible for inclusion within the top 200 in recent Fortune 1000 listings; one would have been ranked in the 600s. We provided each participating company with a statement that outlined our policy of confidentiality, in which we assured the companies that we would not publish, disseminate, or otherwise disclose such information without having aggregated or modified it in such a way as to reasonably protect against association of the identity of the company with the project or with any particular case discussed in the monograph.

After the organization agreed to participate, we conducted a series of discussions with key legal personnel to better understand how the company responds to new requests for e-discovery, learn what steps have been taken in anticipation of those requests, gain insight into the nature and size of the company's IT infrastructure, understand its document-retention policies and disaster-recovery and archiving practices, get a sense of its litigation pressure and the type of cases in which it is involved, and hear what the key challenges in this evolving e-discovery environment were felt to be.

At the outset, we also asked participants to choose a minimum of five cases in which they produced data and electronic documents to another party as part of an e-discovery request. It should be noted that the term *case* as used here covers more than just formally filed suits at law in civil courts and that *e-discovery* covers more than just activities conducted under the FRCP or their state equivalents. Electronic documents can also be produced as part of regulatory inquiries, such as audits or investigations. There can be important differences in the dynamics of electronic-document production when the demanding party is a regulatory agency wielding a civil investigative subpoena rather than a litigation opponent operating under FRCP 34.[23] However, from a technological and logistical standpoint, the process is very similar. Although we were primarily interested in ESI production as part of traditional litigation, we felt that it would be useful to include examples of how companies have responded to the demands of government investigators. Also eligible for inclusion would be binding commercial arbitrations, in

[23] See, e.g., Shonka, 2010.

which the dispute was never a part of a formally filed lawsuit but instead proceeded directly into arbitration as provided for in the language of a contract or other agreement.[24]

As was true with the manner in which we enlisted companies to participate in the research, the selection process for the study cases was not a random one. We requested that each participating company self-select cases that its representative believed to be "recent and representative" of the challenges faced in responding to production demands. Though we had the final say in deciding whether to include any suggested case, there are, of course, selection-bias issues that arise when the subjects of research are given such considerable latitude in shaping the scope and nature of the investigation. We strongly suggested that the cases submitted be closed cases in order to encourage frank and open discussion of what had taken place; that there had not been more than a minimal amount of motion practice related to the discovery event; that no sanctions, spoliation claims, or adverse-inference instructions had been involved; and that the volume of data and the costs incurred could be considered fairly typical of litigation or actions with similar stakes for the participating company. Nevertheless, the initial choice was up to our contacts; in some instances, the characteristics of those cases did not exactly match our suggestions. For example, two cases included in the analysis had discovery-related sanctions, and a few others were being actively litigated at the time we collected ESI production information (and, in fact, remain unresolved as of this writing).

In the end, we received at least some reliable e-discovery production cost data for 57 cases. Forty-five of the cases involved litigation arising from a formally filed lawsuit, one involved a contractual dispute that went directly into binding commercial arbitration, and the remaining 11 were the result of a regulatory investigation. Despite the common association of e-discovery producers as parties on the right-hand side of the "versus" in case titles, a participating company was a plaintiff in 15 cases (in the remainder, the company was a defendant or the target of a civil investigative demand). Some cases included multiple and diverse allegations and defenses, but the primary subject matters of the ones included in the analysis are described in Table 1.1.

The forum within which the discovery was conducted was usually a federal court (36 cases), with nine cases in a state court, 11 cases part of a regulatory investigation, and one handled by commercial arbitrators. The reported stakes in the cases in which we were able to obtain such information ranged from one estimated to be worth \$2 million to another estimated at \$400 million, though some of the regulatory subpoenas involved potential mergers, product defects, or marketing investigations in which the potential monetary impact to the company was likely to be considerably greater. For about half the cases, the bulk of e-discovery activity occurred in 2008; most other cases had e-discovery primarily taking place in 2007 or 2009.

We do not claim that the cases included in our analysis constitute a representative sample of litigations, regulatory enforcements, or commercial arbitrations that involved electronic production by very large corporations. The subjectivity and non–probability-based nature of the selection process counsels against overgeneralizing the results. However, the cases do provide

[24] The rules covering discovery in such situations are a complex mix of contractual language, state arbitration act provisions (if applicable), and the rules of the arbitration provider. As would be true with regulatory investigations, the scope of allowable discovery in arbitrations may well be quite different from the scope of traditional litigation, but the process of collecting and preparing digital information for submission to another party is essentially the same.

Table 1.1
Subject Matter of the Cases Included in the Data Collection

Subject Matter	Cases
Antitrust	2
Contract	8
Employment	1
Environmental	1
Fraud or false claims	4
Insurance	2
Intellectual property	18
Product liability	7
Real property	1
Regulatory investigation	11
Unfair trade practices	2

concrete examples of the resources required to comply with what participating companies of considerable size characterized to us as typical e-discovery requests.

In most instances, once the cases were identified, we held discussions with one or more in-house counsel who were closely associated with the selected litigation for background information on the dispute, the nature of the information or documents sought, the steps taken to respond to the production demand, and the role, if any, that discovery played in the ultimate outcome of the dispute. Personnel from IT departments were often a part of these discussions, as were paralegals: In some instances, the e-discovery production was essentially managed by corporate employees other than attorneys, and, in other instances, such staff had more firsthand knowledge of what had been done. For some of our selected cases, the company had already collected detailed cost data as part of its own independent inquiry into e-discovery expenditures; accordingly, we worked with our contacts to understand the way they had tracked such costs, to fill in any gaps in reporting, and to conform their models for expenditures to what we were using in other example cases.

As we had expected, we encountered informational gaps of one type or another in most of the selected cases. For example, the amount of the data collected or reviewed was sometimes available only when there had been an active effort to track and record such information at the time the case was proceeding. Outside counsel fees specific to activity related to a particular ESI production were often estimated as a percentage of the overall total spent for legal services. Calculating personnel time expenditures within the company itself was a common area of difficulty. When we were given an estimate of IT staff time in terms of days, for example, we had to use Bureau of Labor Statistics (BLS) figures for the average annual salaries for network administrators in the nearest metropolitan area to calculate a daily rate, and then adjusted that rate using other BLS data to reflect total compensation including benefits. A similar approach was taken when we had information only on in-house lawyer time rather than actual compensation. An issue that is discussed in greater detail later involves the potential underreporting of internal expenditures, especially in those cases in which it was asserted (or the data we received suggested) that time spent on the production by staff in the legal or IT departments was negligible. We addressed this issue by testing various scenarios about internal contributions to see how the results might vary. And, in some instances, reported costs might be combined, such as those charged by a single vendor for both collection and processing tasks. If possible, we tried to allocate those expenses based on data provided to us by the company as to the typical breakout of such costs in other cases it had litigated. If it was not possible to make such estimates, then we identified the costs as "unallocated," which meant that they would continue to be a component of the total e-discovery spend even though we could not link them to a specific task or source.

Allocation of Expenditures Across Tasks

The steps involved in responding to a discovery demand for electronic documents may appear to be straightforward (i.e., the request is received, the information requested is assembled, and, ultimately, the data are turned over to the opposing party). However, in actuality, the process is far more complicated. Figure 1.1 represents what is known as the Electronic Discovery Reference Model (EDRM), a conceptual framework for the e-discovery process developed by a group consisting of vendors, attorneys, litigants, and academics involved in e-discovery.[25] The model represents what might be thought of as the nine main stages (or *nodes*) involved in e-discovery preparation, production, and use and was designed to provide standards for the development, evaluation, and use of e-discovery products and services.

Figure 1.1
Electronic Discovery Reference Model

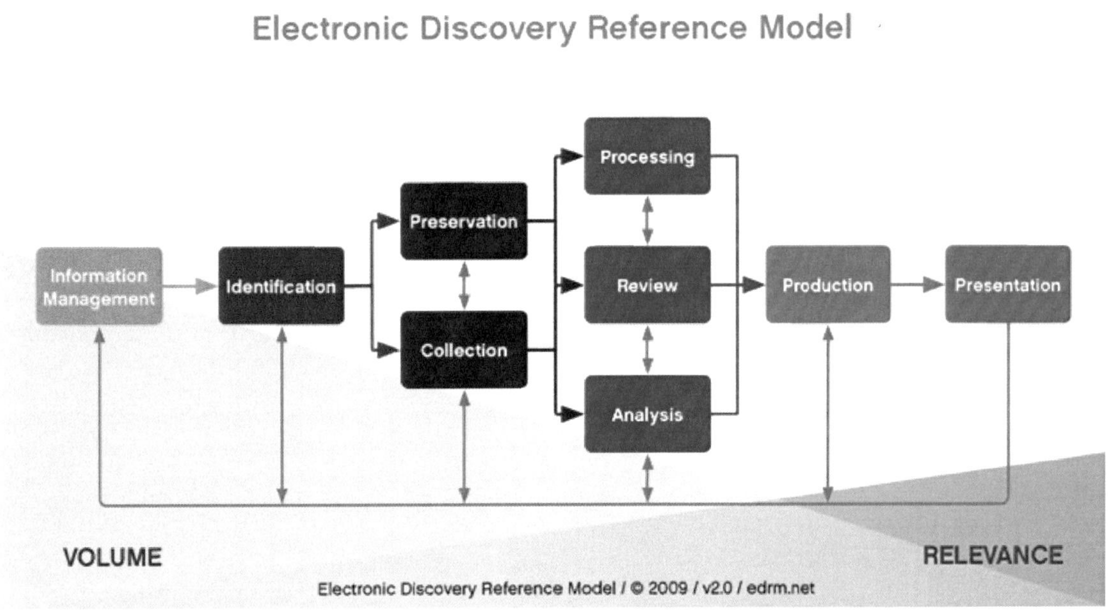

SOURCE: EDRM (edrm.net). Used with permission.
RAND *MG1208-1.1*

[25] For more information on the EDRM group, see EDRM, undated (d).

The following summary provides a brief description of each of the nine nodes of the EDRM:

- *Information management* is managing ESI and IT systems to mitigate risk and expenses in e-discovery, covering the entire process, starting with the creation of ESI through its final disposition.[26] Document-retention and document-destruction policies are prime examples of information governance efforts.
- *Identification* is locating potential sources of ESI and determining its scope, breadth, and depth.[27] This task often involves identifying the "custodians" of potentially relevant information (i.e., people who have the most direct control over the data), "key players" (individuals who are most likely to be associated with documents of interest), and locations (such as specific servers or a set of disaster-recovery backup tapes).
- *Preservation* is ensuring that potentially important ESI is protected against inappropriate alteration or destruction.[28] Steps must be taken to prevent electronic documents that might contain relevant evidence from being significantly altered, lost, or destroyed, regardless of whether such changes would be made intentionally, inadvertently, or in the normal course of business. Preservation duties normally attach when a lawsuit has been initiated or when there is a reasonable anticipation that a lawsuit will be commenced. One common approach to dealing with preservation responsibilities is the issuance of internal *legal holds*, communications to individuals and units within the organization requiring them to take steps to avoid inadvertent or intentional deletion or alteration.[29] Such communications might, for example, inform the recipient to move copies of all emails received or sent between specific dates to a secured network repository; tell key employees to follow a "print-and-retain" policy in which hard copies of emails falling into specific subject-matter categories are created; require the IT department to suspend the routine destruction or overwriting of backup or archiving systems; request that "auto-purge" functions for deleting emails of a certain age left in inboxes be turned off; order a vendor to make mirror-image copies of data on specific desktops or servers; tell a custodian not to disturb data under his or her control; request that the IT department change the files' administrative permissions (such actions are sometimes referred to as a *hold in place* or a *preserve in place*); or request that the security department physically seize specific laptops.[30] Auditing the distribution of the notices and the subsequent level of compliance with the requests is extremely important. Enterprise-level applications have been developed to manage the issuance of legal holds and, in some instances, secure data across multiple platforms and networks. Complicating the preservation process is that the same data can be the subject of multiple legal holds and that certain individuals and types of data can be essentially under what amounts to a "permanent," "open," or "rotating" legal hold.

---

[26] See EDRM, undated (e).

[27] See EDRM, 2010a.

[28] See EDRM, undated (g).

[29] See Sedona Conference, 2010.

[30] For a description of the various approaches taken by organizational litigants to implement legal holds, see Compliance, Governance and Oversight Council and Huron Consulting Group, 2008.

- *Collection* is gathering ESI for further use in the e-discovery process, such as processing or review.[31] Key requirements of the collection process are that it does not inappropriately alter the targeted electronic documents and data, important ESI is not overlooked or missed, and the data's authenticity and chain of custody can be documented. Files are often collected in their "native format" (such as a spreadsheet file created in Microsoft Excel) as a means of maintaining the integrity of "metadata," internal application information (such as the sender's name in an email header or the creation date of the document) stored within a file but apart from a document's primary contents (e.g., the words in the body of an email), as well as external information (such as file size or a description of the subject matter of an image file) stored separately by the application that created the file or the operating system. Collection is accomplished in a variety of ways, such as employing applications to make "forensic-quality" copies (exact bit-by-bit duplication of electronic storage media in a form suitable for presentation in a court of law), using centralized tools that can gather data across different platforms and networks, or through "self-collection," in which the custodians themselves copy targeted ESI to secure repositories or portable devices.
- *Processing* is reducing the volume of ESI and converting it, if necessary, to forms more suitable for review, analysis, and other tasks.[32] Common processing tasks can involve *deduplication* (eliminating multiple copies of essentially the same ESI), dropping administrative and operating-system file types that are known to not contain user-created data, creating versions of the data to be viewed by attorneys and others (e.g., separating attachments from emails, "unzipping" multiple files from compressed versions, subjecting imaged text files to optical character recognition [OCR]), *culling* (zeroing in on the documents that are most likely to be responsive to the demand), reorganizing the document sets in order to increase efficiency during review, or creating indexes (by subject matter or various metadata elements). *Hosting* is the secure storage and management of data after collection. Thus, such tasks as culling or deduplication are performed on hosted data. Hosting also relates to storage services provided postprocessing in conjunction with the use of *review tools*, platforms used during the review phase of the cycle that allow attorneys to view ESI on monitors rather than as individual printouts.
- *Review* is evaluating ESI to identify responsive documents to produce and privileged documents to withhold, gaining a greater understanding of the factual issues in a case, and developing legal strategies based on the type of information that is found in the collection of documents.[33] Traditional practice calls for attorneys to review ESI after collection and processing to confirm that the documents are *responsive* to the scope of the request in the original demand and *relevant* to any of the claims and defenses in the case. Review would also take place to identify whether otherwise-producible documents are *privileged* or *protected* under statute or common law (such as attorney-client communications or materials or other work product prepared by an attorney in anticipation of litigation or trial) and could therefore be withheld from the production. Reviewers might also look for trade secrets or other *highly sensitive* information, which might lead to seeking a pro-

[31] See EDRM, undated (a).

[32] See EDRM, undated (h).

[33] See EDRM, 2010d.

tective order from the court to place the materials under seal and prevent release to the general public. In instances in which documents or sections of documents are identified as privileged or withheld for some other reason, a *privilege log* is created, a type of index describing each item withheld or redacted and the basis for the privilege, protection, or confidentiality claim being asserted. Review can also be done for the purpose of *issue coding* (classifying documents by subject matter or other criteria) or for flagging *hot documents* or *smoking guns* (i.e., documents with the strongest probative value or containing the most-crucial information) to bring to the attention of lead counsel. Reviews are often split into multiple phases; for example, there might be a "first-pass" (or "first-level") review to drop documents that are not both responsive and relevant, and later a "second-pass" (or "second-level") review done by other counsel on the resulting set to identify documents with privileged communications or sensitive information.

- *Analysis* is evaluating one's own ESI for content and context, including the identification of key patterns, topics, people, or discussions.[34] Analytic methodologies may be used for reducing data volume, zeroing in on documents of interest, understanding what the data contain to assist in the producer's own strategic decisions, gauging the productivity of reviewers, helping in identifying other potential sources of responsive ESI, and documenting what took place during collection and processing.
- *Production* is delivering ESI to opposing parties in appropriate forms, using appropriate delivery mechanisms, and in compliance with agreed production specifications and timelines.[35] The exact mechanisms and protocols used for delivering reviewed documents are often the subject of negotiation between the parties in the early stages of discovery, but often the documents are electronically marked with sequential numbers (in a manner similar to traditional Bates numbering) and a separate *load file* is provided (a type of index used by electronic case-management tools popular with many law firms and legal departments).
- *Presentation* is displaying ESI at depositions, hearings, and trials.[36] Both the demanding and producing parties may have the need to present electronic documents and other information to judges, juries, arbitrators, witnesses, and opposing counsel.

In the early stages of our study, we were urged by experts in the field to organize our data collection to conform to all nine phases of the EDRM. However, initial contacts with corporate counsel to review data availability suggested that, for many law departments, costs associated with case-related e-discovery are conceptualized as essentially falling into just three broad areas: *collection*, *processing*, and *review*. It is not that the activities described in the full model do not take place in routine electronic document productions; it is that these three tasks are the ones most often executed by outside entities, such as law firms, vendors, or consultants, and therefore the areas in which expenses have historically been tracked. The distinctions between the formal EDRM and how some corporate counsel view their e-discovery activities may simply be definitional. For example, our background research suggested that, for the litigants we would be contacting, deciding which custodians or databases in the organization

[34] See EDRM, 2010c.

[35] EDRM, 2010b.

[36] EDRM, undated (f).

might have relevant information is often immediately followed by retrieving data from those same sources, both tasks performed by the same individual, department, or outside entity. For such organizations, *identification* of data sources is essentially perceived as a key component of the *collection* process, not as a separate, indivisible step. Although the EDRM provides an extremely nuanced and thoughtful way to understand the overall process, a simpler conceptualization was needed for the type of data collection we hoped to conduct.

The categories of collection, processing, and review we ultimately used to collect cost data are essentially an amalgam of the EDRM's definitions for six of the nine nodes:

- collection
  - locating potential sources of ESI and determining its scope, breadth, and depth following the receipt of a demand to produce electronic documents and data
  - once custodians, key players, and data locations have been identified, gathering ESI for further use in the e-discovery process, such as processing or review, while maintaining data integrity and chain of custody
- processing
  - reducing the volume of collected ESI through automated processing techniques to increase the percentage of documents in the resulting set that are unique, relevant, responsive, and not privileged
  - converting ESI or copying it, if necessary, to forms more suitable for review, analysis, and other tasks
  - hosting the data for performing processing tasks, as well as for use in computerized review applications[37]
  - evaluating and grouping one's own ESI for content and context, including the identification of key patterns, topics, people, or discussions
  - following the completion of the review process, delivering ESI to opposing parties in appropriate forms, using appropriate delivery mechanisms, and in compliance with agreed production specifications and timelines
- review
  - evaluating ESI to identify relevant and responsive documents to produce and privileged documents or information to withhold
  - documenting the review process in order to inform opposing counsel about decisions made regarding privilege, or highly sensitive information
  - Additional goals of the review process are to gain a greater understanding of the factual issues in a case, identify the key documents residing in ESI, and develop legal strategies based on the type of information that is found in the collection of documents.

There are some aspects of e-discovery that we did not include in our study. First, *we did not consider IM in our case-specific cost data collection*. Allocating organizational expenditures for enterprise-wide IM activities to specific production requests would present significant methodological challenges. Second, *presentation was excluded as well*. The presentation of ESI

[37] In some instances, we assigned expenditures for hosting services associated solely with online review to the review category when the task could be determined to be completely separate from processing duties. In actuality, vendors do not always make such distinctions in the services they offer to their clients, and our assumption is that treating all hosting activities as a type of processing would have a negligible effect on aggregate review costs.

at trials and hearings takes place after production and was therefore beyond the scope of this study. Third, *we considered efforts to analyze and evaluate data as part of collection, processing, and review* rather than a stand-alone activity for which reliable expenditure data could be collected. And fourth, although we discuss possible cost issues related to preservation in a separate chapter, *we were unable to collect case-specific information about preservation expenditures in our sample cases.*

Finally, an issue of terminology: Throughout this document, we use the term *production* in the broad sense used in FRCP 34 when it refers to a "Request for Production of Electronically Stored Information." *Production* in this sense means *all* the steps taken to respond to an e-discovery demand, from initial identification of ESI sources to final delivery of the processed and reviewed documents to opposing parties; it is not limited to the final preparations undertaken just before complying with the original request—the definition used in the EDRM framework.

Allocation of Expenditures Across Sources

Following early discussions with participating companies, we felt that it would be most practical to allocate e-discovery expenditures to one of three main sources: outside counsel, vendors and other service providers, and internal corporate staff, including direct expenditures for technology. Each is described in this section.

- *Outside counsel* includes any attorney or law firm retained by the organization to represent its interests (other than its own employees). E-discovery expenses for outside counsel would include hourly billings or other fee arrangements; expenditures managed or controlled by outside counsel, such as those for expert fees, photocopying expenses, and identifiable charges; the use of the firm's IT infrastructure for hosting data; and use of the firm's review-tool platform, travel, and other costs of litigation. One common outside counsel expense involved the law firm's use of contract attorneys (presumably retained only for the specific e-discovery production); we considered such activities to be just another part of the firm's inventory of potential legal services available to its organizational clients. However, it was our preference that expenses only "passing through" outside counsel (such as for the use of offshore discovery services billed to the organization as part of the law firm's invoices) be treated separately (in this example, as a vendor), although this request may not have always been followed. It should be noted that, to the extent possible, we have attempted to exclude outside counsel expenditures related to ancillary proceedings associated with e-discovery generally but not the specific document production of interest. Thus, the costs associated with attendance at an FRCP 26(f) conference to agree to a plan for conducting discovery would not be included in our analysis.
- *Vendors* include companies and individual consultants who offer one or more e-discovery–related services. Such vendors may be selected and managed by outside counsel, in-house counsel, other staff within the organization, or other vendors. One issue that came up was how to classify companies that offer teams of attorneys to provide document review. In one sense, such services parallel those provided by outside counsel because, ultimately, the same legal and ethical relationship exists between the organization and the vendor's legal professional employees as between the organization and temporary attorneys hired either by outside counsel or directly by the corporate legal department. However, such companies are increasingly offering a wide panoply of discovery services in addition to

review, including forensic collection and ESI processing, and offer themselves out as a multifaceted service provider rather than a traditional law firm. As such, we treat such companies as a type of vendor.

- *Internal expenditures* ideally include salaries and benefits paid to the organization's employees, including attorneys, paralegals, and support staff in corporate law departments, as well as members of IT departments and other business units in which effort is expended to comply with e-discovery production requests. Costs associated with contract attorneys directly hired by the corporate legal departments would also be classified as internal expenditures. In addition, purchase costs or licensing fees paid for computer applications and hardware primarily intended to assist in discovery requirements would be included.

Inquiry into Preservation Issues

In the context of e-discovery, preservation involves the legal obligation of organizations and individuals to take steps to prevent the alteration, loss, or destruction of electronic documents that may contain relevant evidence. This duty is not limited to instances in which a formal demand for production has been received but is triggered whenever litigation is reasonably anticipated. To explore the possible cost ramifications of preservation, we held discussions with our main contacts at each company to address issues related to procedures in place to preserve potentially discoverable information, listen to what they felt to be the direct and indirect impacts of preservation, and learn about their concerns in this area. These discussions took place between October 2010 and June 2011.

Our approach here was qualitative in nature because it was clear that gauging the magnitude of preservation expenses in individual cases would present some daunting hurdles. First, the cases already included as part of our inquiry into e-discovery expenditures were all required to have an actual document production, a selection criterion that might provide unrepresentative examples of the many different circumstances in which preservation responsibilities can be in play.[38] Second, even when clearly connected to actual litigation, preservation is a duty that can extend across multiple cases involving the same custodians, files, or data locations, which would make identifying the costs directly related to a specific case speculative at best when the information was subject to a series of cascading and overlapping legal holds. Finally, many organizations do not track their preservation-related expenditures in any systematic way, and we would likely obtain little useful information with the approach we used for production costs, regardless of how cooperative our participants might be. All of these issues suggested that, at least for this phase of our research agenda into e-discovery, our efforts would be best spent understanding litigant behavior and perceptions and the reasons behind their decisions and beliefs rather than attempting to accurately measure preservation costs.

Although we recognize that this approach captures the experiences and opinions of staff at only eight very large organizations, we have no evidence that the main preservation challenges faced by these companies are markedly different from those faced by other companies, large or small. This is not to say that all corporations of this magnitude approach preservation requirements in the same way (indeed, there is considerable divergence in preservation practices across our participating companies), but the underlying concerns about preservation and legal holds should be fairly similar.

---

[38] A recent survey of attorneys suggests that demands for the production of ESI are made in less than half of cases with any discovery at all (Lee and Willging, 2009, p. 1).

Study Limitations

It should be noted that this inquiry does not consider the costs that can be incurred by the parties *propounding* e-discovery requests. Nor did we attempt to contact the lawyers and litigants opposing the participating companies in the sample cases for an *alternative perspective* on e-discovery costs and issues for the productions in question. We also did not try to measure the per-case costs that are *indirectly* associated with e-discovery production, perhaps most notably those connected with preservation duties. We also exclude from our inquiry costs that may arise from adapting or shaping *organizational practices* in light of current e-discovery realities (for example, productivity losses resulting from a decision to not provide employees with instant-messaging capabilities because of preservation concerns). Discovery *events of relatively modest size* were generally not included.[39] The organizational litigants participating in the study include some of the largest corporations in the United States, so the *experiences of relatively small companies* were not included. And finally, the approach we have taken also ignores the *benefits of discovery* in the search for truth, in helping to narrow issues in anticipation of trial, and in providing sufficient information to both sides of a dispute in order for the parties to realistically assess their respective chances before a trier of fact.

Organization of This Monograph

In the rest of this monograph, we present the results of our analysis of the four research questions. In Chapter Two, we describe the costs of collecting, processing, and reviewing electronic information. In Chapter Three, we break down those costs by the source of expenditure: internal organizational resources, vendors, and outside counsel. In the subsequent two chapters, we explore several approaches to reducing the costs of review, the most expensive task in producing electronic documents. Chapter Four discusses limits within the current model of review on reducing the cost of labor or increasing the speed with which lawyers review documents. We also summarize the evidence from studies assessing the quality of traditional review approaches. Chapter Five examines the savings that can be achieved by moving beyond traditional review to adopt processes by which a computer, rather than an attorney, determines whether documents are relevant, responsive, or privileged and describes what we know about how the quality of such approaches compares with that in traditional review. Chapter Six identifies the barriers to adopting such computerized methodologies and offers some ideas for surmounting those barriers. Chapter Seven describes what we learned from our interviews about the costs of preservation, the uncertainty surrounding preservation duties, and the need for clearer guidance about how preservation should be conducted. In the final chapter, we summarize our findings and make several recommendations to address the main issues identified in the analysis.

Additional material can be found in the appendixes. Appendix A contains additional tables presenting the findings on e-discovery production costs found in Chapters Two and Three. Appendix B provides explanatory material for important statistical measures used in many information-retrieval studies.

---

[39] More than half of all cases with some information on volume involved either the collection, processing, or review of at least 100 gigabytes of data.

CHAPTER TWO

Production Expenditures, by Task

In this chapter, we examine how production costs in our sample cases break out by collection, processing, and review.

Total Costs of Production

Though it is not possible to assess the extent to which the cases included in our data collection actually reflect typical e-discovery production in the participating companies as we had requested, total expenditures do range from a seemingly modest $17,000 (in an intellectual property matter) to $27 million (in a product-liability case), with a median value of $1.8 million (see Table 2.1). Note that we were able to calculate total spend for ESI production in only 45 of the 57 cases for which we sought cost data. As is apparent in the tables and figures in this chapter, there were gaps in the information available to us that prevented applying the same set of metrics to all 57 cases. Some of the 12 cases missing from Table 2.1 might not, for example,

Table 2.1
Production Costs for 45 Cases

Subject Matter	Total Cost ($)
Intellectual property	17,183
Government subpoena	22,810
Product liability	38,743
Intellectual property	76,950
Intellectual property	82,478
Insurance	147,004
Government subpoena	186,692
Government subpoena	187,979
Fraud or false claims	252,473
Intellectual property	275,394
Contract	307,587
Intellectual property	328,405
Contract	334,372

Table 2.1—Continued

Subject Matter	Total Cost ($)
Intellectual property	432,588
Intellectual property	573,365
Intellectual property	708,016
Intellectual property	718,083
Government subpoena	788,928
Government subpoena	1,173,685
Contract	1,266,457
Intellectual property	1,324,597
Fraud or false claims	1,329,891
Government subpoena	1,770,715
Intellectual property	1,969,971
Product liability	2,031,138
Intellectual property	2,076,257
Intellectual property	2,150,000
Antitrust	2,169,189
Product liability	2,198,006
Product liability	2,210,724
Government subpoena	2,489,165
Intellectual property	2,541,383
Fraud or false claims	2,623,693
Government subpoena	3,007,116
Intellectual property	3,186,587
Fraud or false claims	3,208,863
Government subpoena	3,426,014
Contract	4,042,606
Product liability	4,418,022
Government subpoena	5,133,422
Employment	6,974,027
Intellectual property	7,803,064
Antitrust	8,367,649
Product liability	21,007,504
Product liability	27,118,520

have complete information about the costs of review or for all expenses associated with vendors, so we could not calculate the total spend for responding to requests for production.

Most of the cases included in our data collection involved discovery expenditures that were much larger than what a recent Federal Judicial Center (FJC) survey reported as the median total litigation expenditures of producing parties in a sample of federal cases.[1] The cost data presented in this monograph should be considered in light of the fact that the scope of production was atypical compared with that of the "average" case described in the FJC study. But total expenditures in and of themselves mean little in interpreting whether the costs of production were justified by the unique circumstances of the case, such as monetary claims made by the plaintiffs, the probative value of the information produced, or particular challenges faced during collection, processing, or review. We did attempt to collect information about stakes, but the results were judged to be unacceptable due to difficulties in applying a uniform definition for litigation value. For example, the stakes in one case were estimated by our organizational contact to be worth tens of millions of dollars if only the instant litigation were considered, but many hundreds of millions more based on that litigation's potential to disrupt the company's other lines of business if resulting media coverage was unfavorable or if a successful outcome for the opposing party spawned a rash of similar claims. The stakes associated with regulatory investigations were particularly difficult to determine. Some of the participating companies' representatives were quite frank in describing how they approached the problem of balancing e-discovery expenditures against the apparent stakes in a case, reporting that they would not shy away from committing what might seem to be a disproportional amount of resources to comply with an electronic-document demand if they believed that the claims against them were of questionable merit or the damages sought were grossly exaggerated.[2]

Perhaps a more useful way to view these cases is by the costs incurred for each gigabyte (GB) of what was actually turned over to the other side after collection, processing, and review were completed, as shown in Figure 2.1 (for a detailed list of cases presented in that figure, along with their primary subject matters, see Table A.1 in Appendix A). For most cases in our study group, those costs were less than $40,000 per gigabyte, and, for about one-third of the cases, less than $20,000. However, in one instance, the company spent $900,000 to produce an amount of data that would consume less than one-quarter of the available capacity of an ordinary DVD.[3] Arguably, it is not the volume of the production that matters but what it contained in terms of the data's intrinsic value (for example, the degree to which the data help provide all litigants with mutual knowledge of relevant facts). Such an analysis was beyond the scope of this monograph. Some cases in our collection did reach the trial stage, though the extent to which any e-discovery was transformed into admitted evidence and presented to the trier of fact is unknown.

The numbers are somewhat more consistent across cases when the focus is on the total costs per gigabyte reviewed. Arguably, gigabytes reviewed provides a more useful way of com-

---

[1] Lee and Willging, 2009, Tables 4 and 5.

[2] We were confident of both the estimated stakes and total spend in just six instances. In four of those six cases, final production expenditures were 3 percent or less of case value; in a fifth, it was about 16 percent. In the remaining case, e-discovery expenditures were roughly about the same as the apparent monetary stakes in the case, but an adverse outcome in that particular litigation was said to have important implications for other actions in which the company was involved.

[3] The discussion concerns costs per gigabyte of data. In actuality, the case discussed involved a production of about 3.5 gigabytes of data in total, with total e-discovery–related expenditures of about $3.2 million.

Figure 2.1
Total Costs per Gigabyte Produced, 32 Cases

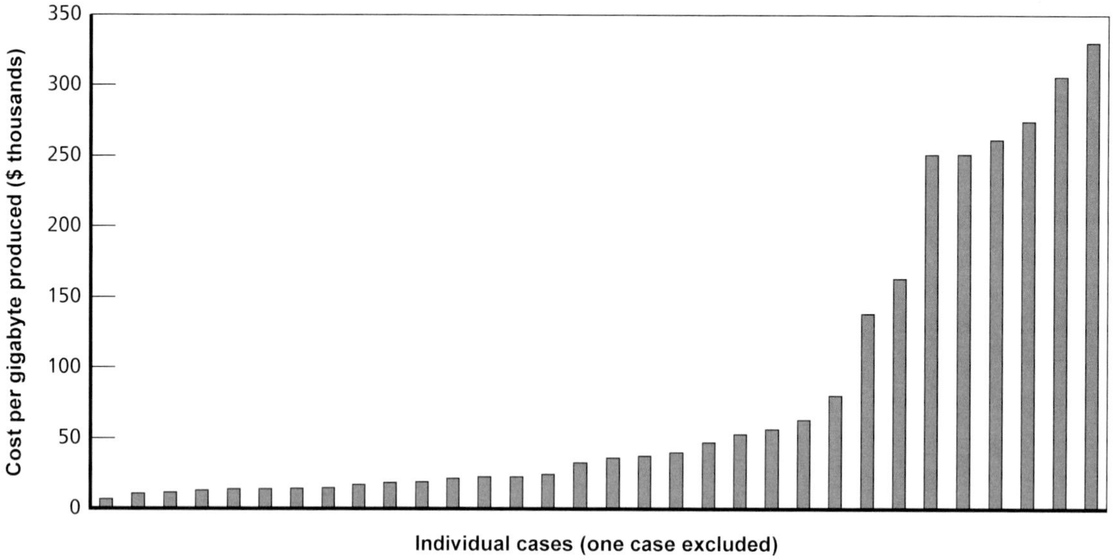

NOTE: The figure excludes one case in which costs per gigabyte produced were greater than $350,000.
RAND *MG1208-2.1*

paring the e-discovery process across cases because, at least in theory, the review stage is not primarily intended as a tool to reduce volume. Documents may be excluded from production because of concerns about privilege or a determination that they are not relevant and responsive. However, it is arguable that the "success" of a review is not measured by how many documents or gigabytes of data were ultimately withheld. As can be seen in Figure 2.2, the total costs per gigabyte reviewed were generally around $18,000, with the first and third quartiles in the 35 cases with complete information at $12,000 and $30,000, respectively.[4] There was one instance in which total costs for each gigabyte of data reviewed was $358,000; it appears that this case was subjected to an especially vigorous review effort using both outside counsel and offshore vendors, resulting in a final production that was just 40 percent of the volume of the reviewed data.

Costs of Collection

As the e-discovery world began to mature in the 1990s and early 2000s, many of the leading opinions and rule-making efforts during that period focused on issues of collection. Locating specific emails on disaster-recovery backup tapes that may not be in reasonably accessible formats, pulling files off inactive servers, accessing legacy computer systems, and sifting through metadata dominated the fact patterns of important court rulings and stakeholder complaints. But, in more-recent times, as represented by Figure 2.3, collection generally consumes less than 10 percent of total e-discovery expenditures.[5] There are exceptions, as can be seen in the right

[4] See also Table A.2 in Appendix A.

[5] See also Table A.3 in Appendix A.

Figure 2.2
Total Costs per Gigabyte Reviewed, 35 Cases

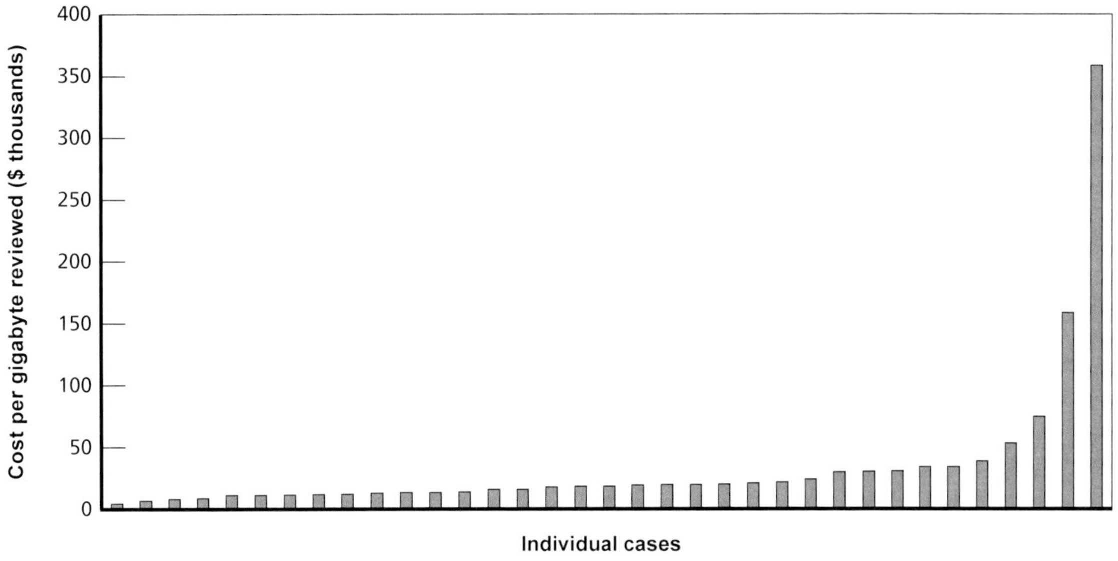

RAND *MG1208-2.2*

Figure 2.3
Distribution of Cases by Percentage of Total Costs Consumed by Collection, 44 Cases

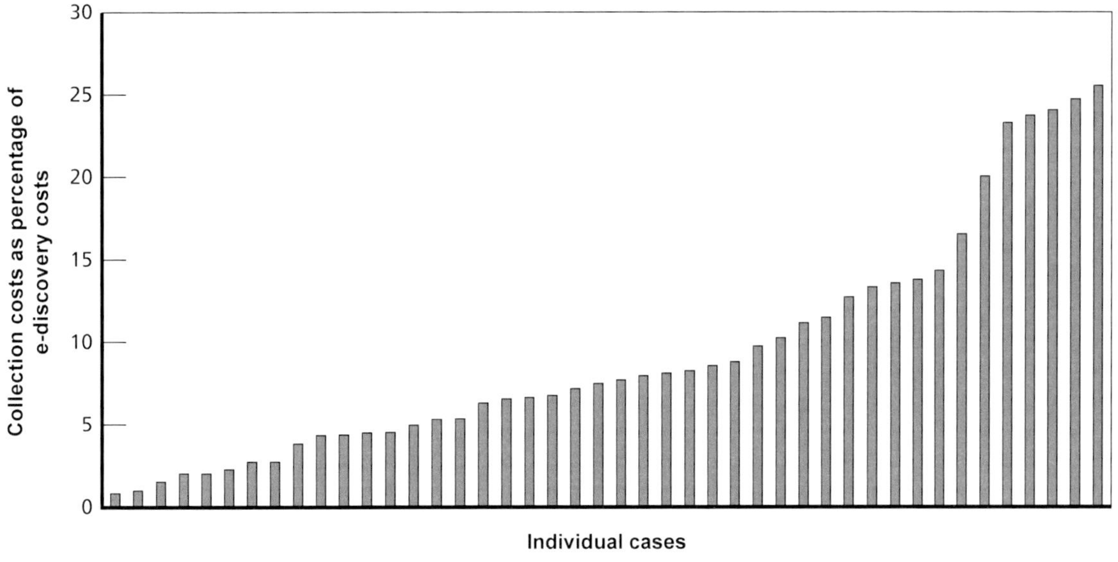

RAND *MG1208-2.3*

side of Figure 2.3, in which four of the 44 cases with complete information in this regard have collection costs constituting nearly one-fourth of total spend. However, in most instances, collection was not the primary consumer of e-discovery costs.

Discussions with the representatives of the participating companies suggest that organizations generally have the fewest problems (in other words, incur the smallest expense-to-volume ratio) when the target of their collection efforts consists of what was described as "active" data created and modified in the ordinary course of business and stored on fixed resources. These would include end user–controlled application files on an office desktop, such as documents created using Corel WordPerfect or Microsoft Word, or emails centrally stored on a networked server. It would also include business record–oriented information, which was described as perhaps the most-accessible data of all because the source databases, unlike unstructured or dispersed data, such as emails, are usually well-defined structures with good indexes and documentation and singular locations. Collection of active data was done either through physically accessing the device (e.g., visiting the office where the computer is located and connecting a portable drive) or through centralized collection tools that can reach across a network and copy data across connected devices. More difficult to access, at least in the experience of most of our contacts, would be active data stored outside the direct control of the organization, such as on portable laptop computers or smart phones. These require coordinating the collection with the employee assigned to the device, which presented particularly difficult challenges in one of the sample cases because of scheduling conflicts and reluctance on the employees' part to separate themselves from their primary tools for conducting business for a day or more. The level of expenses incurred was said to ramp up considerably in instances in which the ESI sought was data other than active business files (for example, deleted information or hidden files) because doing so required specialized forensic tools and expertise that most participating companies did not possess at the time of our research.

In a few of our cases, considerable expense was incurred for collecting from archival sources—in one instance, requiring a forensic-level search of backup tapes for possibly deleted emails, with tens of thousands of tapes pulled out of rotation. Such archiving systems were described to us by one participant as "business efficient, not litigation efficient," primarily designed for emergencies rather than searching and retrieving specific files, a process characterized as "neither fast nor cheap." But legacy systems appear to have presented the greatest challenges. It is common in organizations of the size included in our study to have merged or absorbed other corporate entities over time, sometimes resulting in significant computer-system compatibility issues and the inability to effectively work with proprietary applications that were designed or operated by staff who are no longer available. Converting legacy information into a form that can be examined on the current systems available to the company also increases costs. In one case reported to us, despite extensive use of third-party consultants to read a system once used by a company that was no longer in existence, the legacy computer application was of such an outmoded design that it was essentially impossible to produce native-file versions of the information stored; ultimately, the only solution was to print out millions of hard-copy documents. Even with such issues, however, collection costs were no more than 14 percent of the total electronic document production spend.

The relatively low proportion of total spend for collection in most cases is intriguing because, at the time discovery was conducted in our sample cases, for the most part, participant companies were not employing centralized collection tools. These tools are quite powerful, providing an automated collection process across the company's internal network without directly interrupting work being performed by a targeted custodian or data location, but they require a fairly significant up-front investment of money and labor (one estimate given to us for a participating company's impending adoption of a popular collection tool was about \$500,000 for the initial purchase and an anticipated \$500,000 for labor costs for training and use) and are only now becoming standard in large enterprises.[6] In most of the cases shown in Figure 2.3, the companies approached the problem of collection in more-traditional ways, such as collecting data from each computer or server individually. This would be especially true in situations in which central email services might contain a maximum of only 100 megabytes or so of current messages for each employee, with all archived messages residing in each employee's assigned computer. The precise manner in which information was collected varied both across companies and across cases within the companies. In some instances, hard drives were imaged using forensic copying tools; in others, the collection was far more straightforward, with the use of commands, such as "robocopy," that simply make copies of active files without necessarily preserving all metadata. In many instances, the employees themselves were responsible for self-collection, "dragging and dropping" identified files and folders into a centralized repository. The specific decision to employ one method or another appears to be dependent on the seriousness of the case (however defined), the number of potential custodians or locations, the potential for challenges to the manner in which the data were preserved, and what was described to us as the "reasonableness" of opposing counsel.[7]

Though many of the cases involved collection from specific locations rather than from individual custodians, it may be helpful to look at collection costs on a per-custodian basis. The spread from the first quartile to the third was about $700 to $3,700 in the 35 cases with reported data, with the median at about $1,500 (see Figure 2.4).[8]

Costs of Processing

Reducing the volume of ESI through such techniques as deduplication, hosting the data on servers, or putting the information in a form that assists in subsequent review or analysis can be a major cost driver for e-discovery expenditures—especially when that effort is increased in the face of potentially large review costs. However, in three-fourths of the 44 cases reporting, processing costs were 26 percent or less of total spend (see Figure 2.5).[9] There were, however, seven instances in which the percentage was 40 percent or more and ten cases in which it was less than 10 percent. The leftmost case in Figure 2.5 (the first listed in Table A.5 in Appendix A) was reported to us as having negligible processing costs, which may be a function of the manner in which the data were originally collected, resulting in a narrowly targeted set of documents at the outset of the production cycle.

---

[6] Costs are only one consideration in deciding whether to adopt an automated, enterprise-level collection tool. How computing resources are distributed across a company and the diversity of various platforms used by employees may work against finding a cost-effective solution using such tools. One company now using such a tool reported that the process, although automated, can be much slower than a manual approach because generally the collecting tool examines every file and database in a system, which may not be as efficient as simply asking employees to self-collect documents of a particular topic or type. Another participating company reported that, because of European privacy laws, it could not always use its networked tool when collecting from its overseas operations.

[7] It should also be noted that, for the period when discovery was being conducted in our sample cases, none of the companies reported that it was using computing resources distributed over the Internet (*cloud computing*) for managing its email requirements, an approach that was claimed by one participant as a potential means of reducing company costs of both collection and preservation. One participating company was in the process of moving in that direction.

[8] See also Table A.4 in Appendix A.

[9] See also Table A.5 in Appendix A.

Figure 2.4
Distribution of Cases by Per-Custodian Collection Costs, 35 Cases

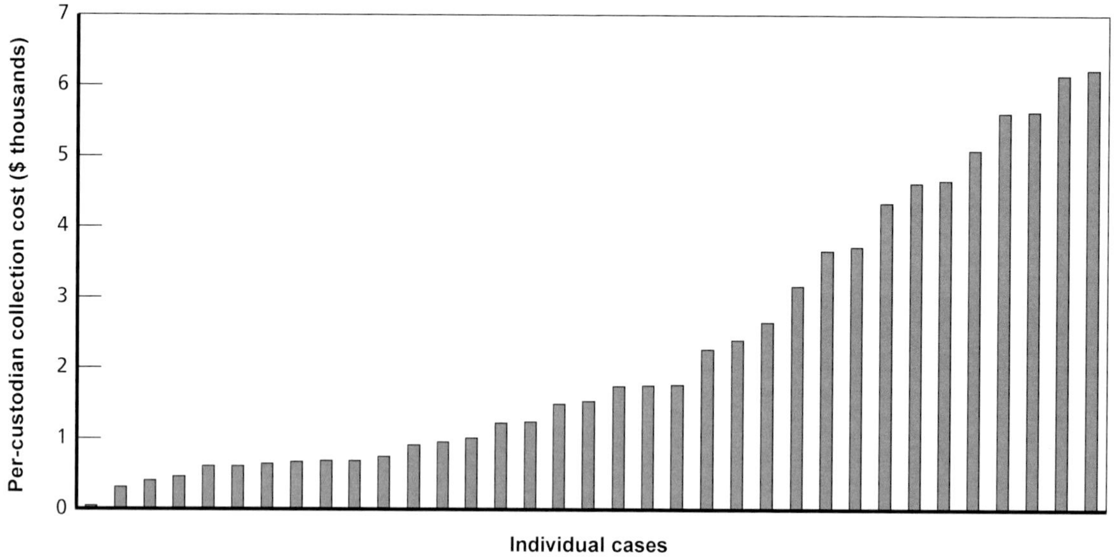

RAND *MG1208-2.4*

Figure 2.5
Distribution of Cases by Percentage of Total Costs Consumed by Processing, 44 Cases

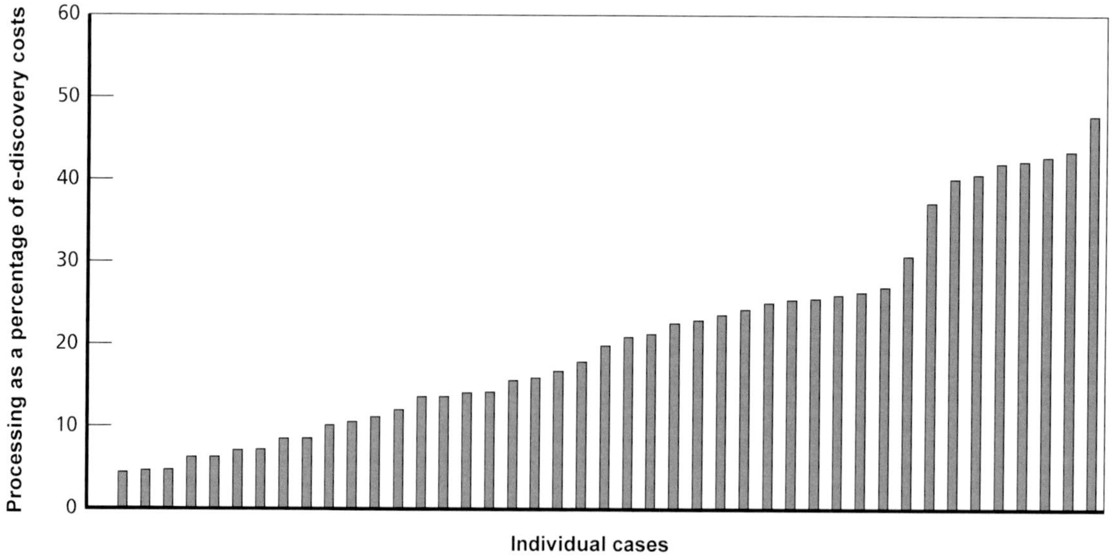

RAND *MG1208-2.5*

Processing appears to be a category of tasks that the participants in our data collection were traditionally reluctant to bring in-house. A typical description of how it was accomplished involved outside counsel recommending one or more vendors to handle processing-related chores, even if collection had been performed mostly using internal resources. Vendors might also be used for hosting data on a platform for the purposes of review, though generally the actual review would be done by others. The specific approaches such vendors might have used to perform deduplication, cull, extract metadata, or other tasks in the study cases are unknown.

Costs of Review

As Figure 2.6 illustrates, the major cost driver in our cases was the review for relevance, responsiveness, and privilege.[10] Although there were cases in which review constituted less than half of the total spend, more than half of the 44 cases with sufficient information had the review percentage at 70 percent or more.

It should be noted that it was not always clear whether hosting and online review platform services were inadvertently included in the expenditures reported for review. Our approach sought to classify such expenses as a type of processing task, but there were instances in which fees and expenses paid to outside counsel may have covered such services to some unknown degree. In most cases, the distinction was straightforward because the vendor performing processing tasks was also responsible for hosting and provision of an online review tool.

Generally, our participating companies reported that the review was split into a first pass to confirm the relevance and responsiveness of the processed ESI and a second pass through the confirmed set in order to identify whether the documents might be privileged (and therefore could be withheld) or contained sensitive information (and therefore might have needed redaction of passages or protective orders). Approaches varied, both across companies and across cases within companies, in terms of who might be responsible for each pass. One reported

Figure 2.6
Distribution of Cases by Percentage of Total Costs Consumed by Review, 44 Cases

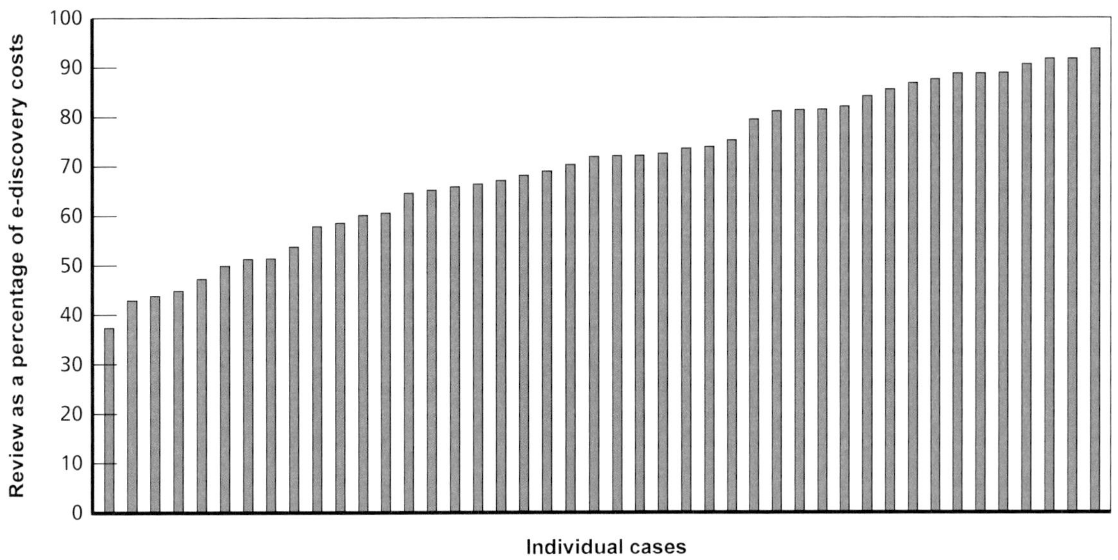

RAND *MG1208-2.6*

---

[10] See also Table A.6 in Appendix A.

practice involved using two different law firms. One company described its preferred firm for first-pass review as one having "a stable of contract attorneys with a relatively cheap rate," with a higher-priced firm used for the second pass on the assumption that the volume of ESI would have been reduced dramatically by that point and a more experienced eye needed. Rates reported for these two species of firms varied, but they usually were between $110 and $175 per hour for the less expensive first-pass attorneys and between $225 and $300 (but sometimes more) for the second-pass lawyers.

The standard method at another participating company was to conduct the first-pass review in-house using contract attorneys hired and managed directly by the company. It was reported that the hourly costs for such temporary lawyers could be as low as $40 to $50 once the process of maintaining a cadre of contract attorneys was integrated into the company's normal course of business. A related approach was used by companies that sent ESI to vendors that offer first-pass attorney review services, either through contract attorneys managed by the vendor or through permanent staff attorneys. When the attorneys used by the vendors were based in the United States, costs for such services were usually estimated at around $50 to $70 per hour. The use of offshore attorneys by such vendors, however, can drop that per-hour rate by about half, though some offshore providers had reportedly moved to a per-document pricing structure.

Still another approach involved the use of the legal department's own staff attorneys for the first pass (and an outside firm for the second) when the subject of the collected ESI involved particularly sensitive topics or senior custodians; doing so was said to avoid the potential risks of disclosing business-critical or highly strategic information to temporary contract attorneys, external vendors, or low-level law firm associates, though the costs of such an approach can be considerable: "When you get 60 to 70 custodians with up to 30 gigs [gigabytes] of email, it takes a lot of time for senior management to review each message." One company reported that it generally uses a single law firm for all review tasks in a case but that, because of the nature of its caseload and its particular approach to preservation and collection, the proportion of nonrelevant or nonresponsive documents sent to outside counsel would be quite small. And finally, in one instance, it was reported that, because the unique circumstances of the case warranted the most streamlined approach possible, an eyes-on approach to the first-pass review was discarded in favor of one that exclusively used search terms to identify potentially relevant and responsive documents that were not clearly privileged, which were then subject to a formal review for privileged communications or sensitive information.

The variations in approaches taken here reflect participants' concerns about what are felt to be the very high costs of review, compared with the other aspects of the e-discovery production cycle, which several of our interviewees believed to have diminished in cost in recent years. As one company representative put it, "It's the second-line review that kills us, the one for privilege; some firms try to charge us $320 per hour for using third-year associates for this sort of work." Another company was moving toward a three-tiered solution, one in which advanced search and data-mining techniques will be used identify the files that are the most likely to be relevant, responsive, and nonprivileged; a second pass by relatively inexpensive paralegals used to cull the data to a minimum; and a third pass to be done by outside counsel (none of the cases in our sample appears to have been subjected to such a process). Ultimately, the decision as to how to approach review has a great effect on total e-discovery production expenditures, but the decision is not always one based solely on economics. One participant explained that the company's discovery costs are not necessarily tied to size or volume of the case; a small matter in terms of data to be reviewed might have substantive issues that require a very thorough examination of each document with the highest quality of reviewer available, while there are other cases that the company would "just throw offshore" because the low potential for risk and exposure does not justify significant expense.

Volume Produced Compared with Volume Collected

A natural question that arises is how much of an effect tasks associated with processing and review had on the mass of information collected at the outset of the production cycle. Although the answer may seem quite straightforward, measuring such changes does present methodological challenges. Electronic information often undergoes transformation to new forms and new formats in different steps of the process and may even expand as additional files are created to present information in a manner more amenable to manipulation or searching. A file containing an imaged version of the text of an email, for example, may be much larger than the original file. Data volume could also increase from point to point if much of the collected ESI was originally in a compressed format. Perhaps a more useful way to discuss the winnowing of ESI from one stage to another would be in terms of documents or individual pages (or images), but data volume in terms of bytes appears to be the most commonly tracked metric of the amount of "work" required or performed.

In the 36 cases in which we were able to obtain information on both the volume collected and the volume ultimately produced, the median reduction in volume was 34 percent, with the lower and upper quartiles at 9 percent and 78 percent, respectively. But much of what was observed here may be a function of the scope of collection rather than of the manner in which data volume is reduced through processing or review. An aggressive effort to identify the minimum number of custodians, data locations, or file types most likely to control or contain relevant and responsive data could conceivably result in a relatively low reduction from collection volume to production volume. In contrast, a company might err heavily on the side of caution by choosing to overcollect, or collect more data than it actually expects to need, with greater reliance on the processing methodologies to significantly cull the collected data. Concerns about preservation requirements and the potential for sanctions for failure to prevent loss of data that may be relevant to current or future litigation may also increase the volume of data at the front end of the process. In such instances, the reduction percentage would be higher, even though the amount of data actually produced could be about the same in both examples.[11]

Unit Costs for Production Tasks

Table 2.2 illustrates how costs for various stages in the e-discovery production cycle can vary, even when adjusted for the amount of data subjected to a particular task. On a per-gigabyte

[11] An example of such a relatively conservative approach to the initial stages of the production cycle comes from a corporation publicly reporting that the average case it litigates involves 48,431,250 pages of preserved data, 12,915,000 pages of data collected and processed, 645,750 pages reviewed, and 141,450 pages actually produced (Howard, Palmer, and Banks, 2011, p. 5). The average reduction from pages collected and processed to pages produced would be 99 percent. To the extent that the page metric translates into a uniform volume of data in terms of bytes, the 99-percent value would be at the upper extreme in the spread of data reductions observed in the 36 cases in our study with such information.

Table 2.2
Unit Costs for Production Tasks

Measure	Collection Costs per Gigabyte Collected	Processing Costs per Gigabyte Processed	Review Costs per Gigabyte Reviewed
Median ($)	940	2,931	13,636
Lower quartile ($)	410	1,157	10,043
Upper quartile ($)	1,767	3,224	19,455
Mean ($)	1,332	2,793	22,480
Minimum ($)	125	598	1,766
Maximum ($)	6,706	6,069	209,899
Number of cases included	29	9	36

basis, costs for collection ranged from $125 to $6,700, from $600 to $6,000 for processing, and from $1,800 to $210,000 for review. The differences between the first and third quartiles for these values, one way to look at the spread in possible costs, reflect a high degree of variation. For collection, the third-quartile measure for per-gigabyte costs was slightly more than four times the size of the first quartile; for processing and review, the multipliers were just under three and two, respectively. Though gathering information on volume at various stages of the production cycle proved difficult, especially for the amount of data subject to processing (with just nine cases reported with per-gigabyte processing costs, the distributions for the amounts reported are highly suspect), the limited results available do suggest that costs at every stage are anything but uniform across cases.

It should be kept in mind that there are certainly guidelines routinely used by e-discovery vendors to estimate their potential costs for proposed efforts on behalf of clients based on the number of custodians, documents, emails, or file sizes for whatever task they have been asked to bid.[12] Such estimations, however, presumably reflect the vendors' experiences, the methods intended to be employed in the proposed work, and the specific characteristics of the data requiring outside services. A vendor's rough estimate for the costs of collecting 10 GB of data each from ten custodians at a single company, for example, might differ markedly for a subsequent collection effort, even for the same company, the same number of custodians, and the same assumed collection size. As such, it does not seem to be possible to speak of e-discovery costs in a way that would allow reliable predictions of total expenditures for any particular production demand using a one-size-fits-all model. The companies with whose representatives we spoke differed markedly in their IT structures, corporate organizations, e-discovery approaches, hold policies, vendor choices, relationships with outside counsel, and many other aspects that all seemed to play a role in driving what the final cost numbers looked like. Just as it is true that there is not one uniform case processing speed in courts across the nation because local legal culture varies from location to location, there does not seem to be a uniform relationship between data volume and final costs, varying instead by the unique aspects of opposing counsel's demand and the capabilities, practices, and risk-related judgments of the producing party. Thus, it would be unwise for a judge, for example, to presume that the costs

[12] See, e.g., Orange Legal Technologies, undated.

of production in a case before the court would reflect the same relationship to data volume or custodians as was observed in other litigation.

It would, however, be misleading to imply that data volume and production costs are completely unrelated. Figure 2.7 plots total production expenses by the number of gigabytes of data collected at the outset of the cycle for the 29 cases for which both types of information were reported. Generally, as collection size increases, so does the final total for production. However, as can be more easily seen in Figure 2.8, the trend flattens somewhat for a set of cases in which 250 to 500 gigabytes were collected.

Another commonly used predictor of total costs is the number of custodians included in the original collection effort (Figure 2.9). Though the obvious relationship presented in Figure 2.8 for collected volume and final costs is not repeated in Figure 2.9, custodian count does appear to play a role. It should be noted that, for the sake of clarity, Figure 2.9 excludes two cases with much-larger final production costs or custodian counts than others with complete information. One involved 544 custodians with a final spend of about $27 million, while the other case, with 640 custodians, resulted in a far more modest $1.3 million in total estimated e-discovery production costs.

Not surprisingly given the dominance of the review process in terms of total e-discovery spend (see Figure 2.6), there certainly appears to be a relationship between the volume of data subject to review and final costs. Both Figure 2.10 and Figure 2.11 illustrate how review volume and total expenditures are correlated, with the top three cases in terms of review volume excluded in Figure 2.11 in order to better present the relationship when the volume was less than 300 GB.

Figure 2.7
How the Volume of Data Collected Is Related to the Total Cost of Production, 29 Cases

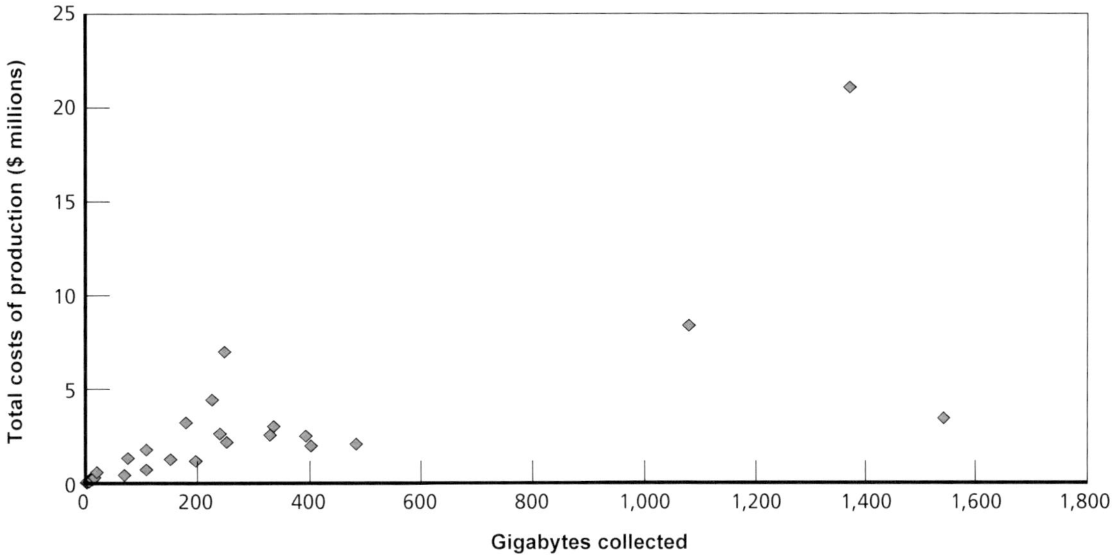

RAND *MG1208-2.7*

Figure 2.8
How the Volume of Data Collected Is Related to the Total Cost of Production, Largest-Volume Cases Excluded, 26 Cases

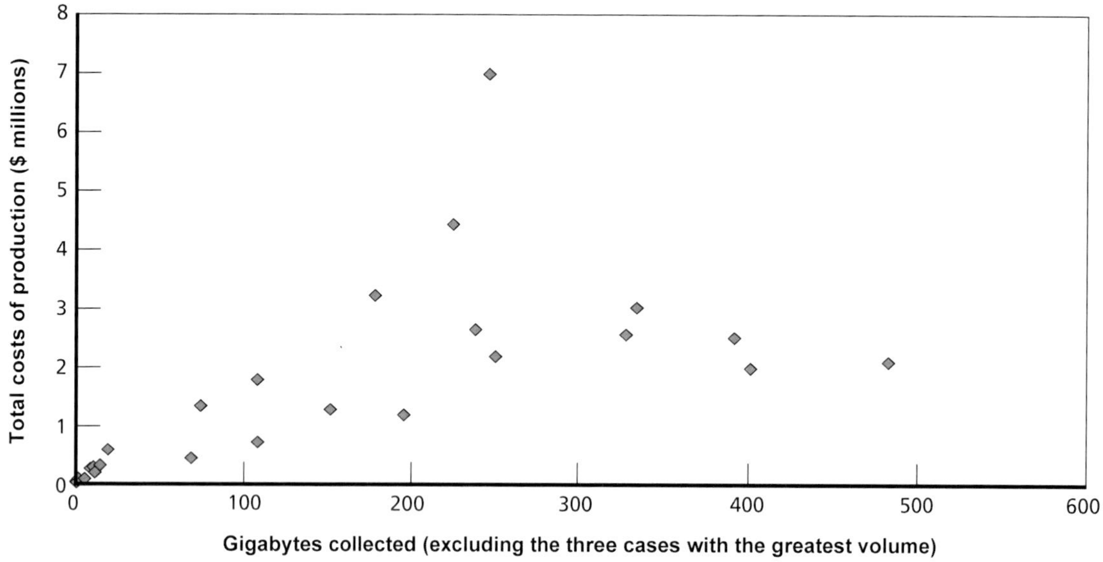

RAND *MG1208-2.8*

Figure 2.9
How the Number of Custodians Included Is Related to the Total Cost of Production, Largest–Custodian-Count Cases Excluded, 33 Cases

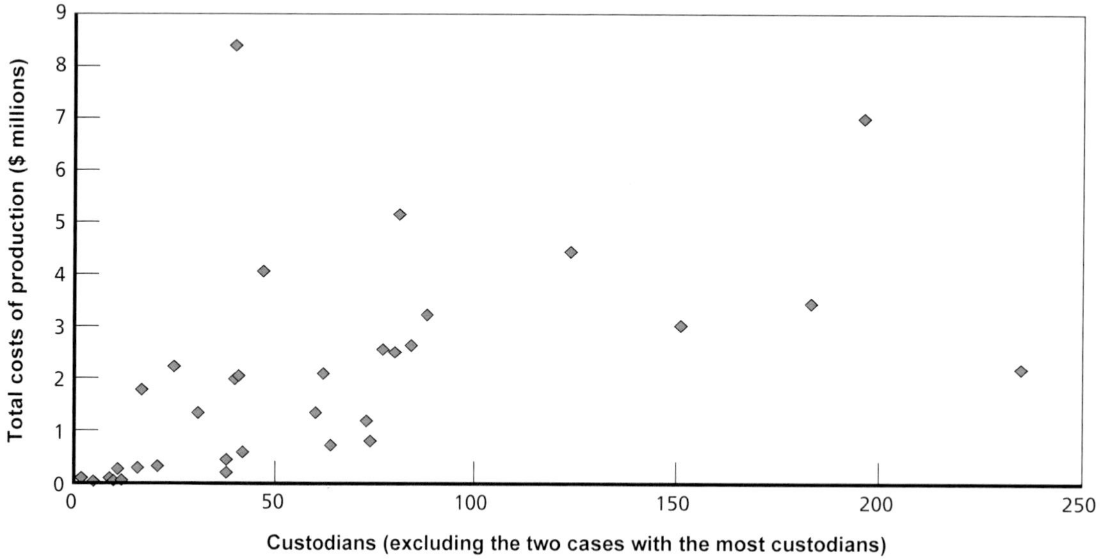

RAND *MG1208-2.9*

Figure 2.10
How the Volume of Data Reviewed Is Related to the Total Cost of Production, 35 Cases

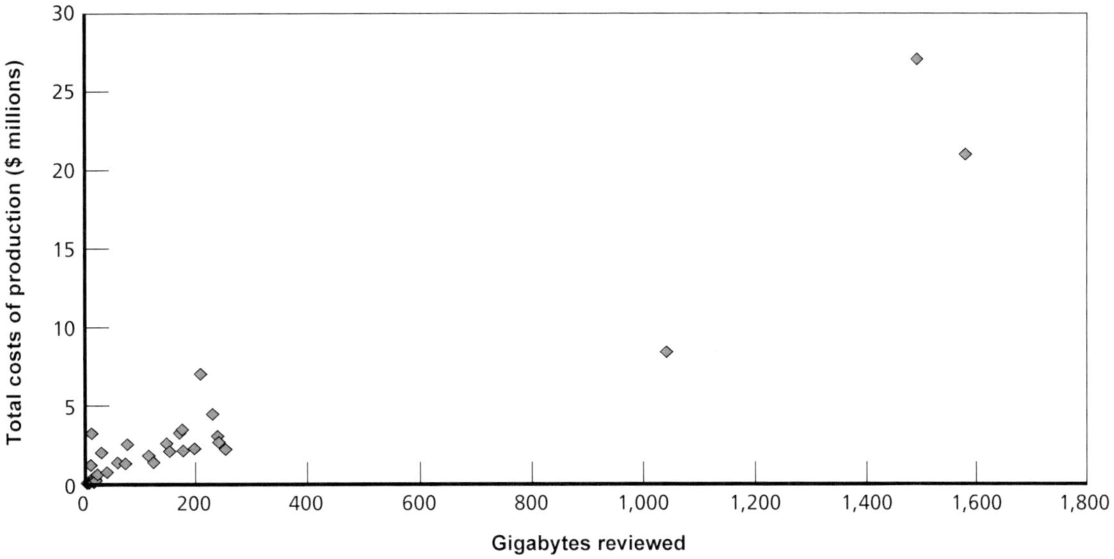

RAND *MG1208-2.10*

Figure 2.11
How the Volume of Data Reviewed Is Related to the Total Cost of Production, Largest-Volume Cases Excluded, 32 Cases

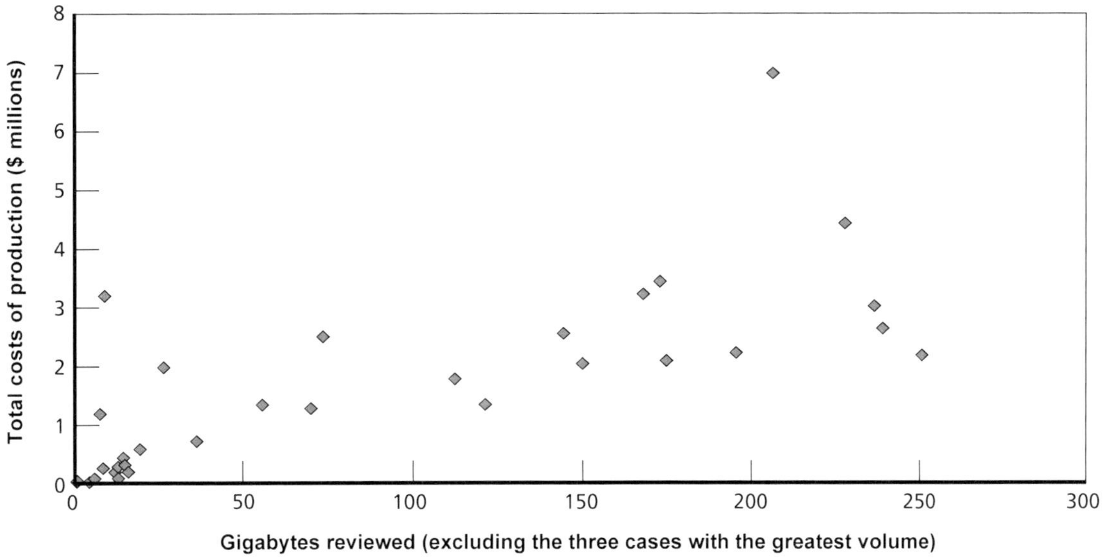

RAND *MG1208-2.11*

CHAPTER THREE

Sources of Expenditures

In this chapter, we present our findings on the costs of producing e-discovery by the source of expenditure, such as internal organizational resources, vendors, or outside counsel. At the end of the chapter, we explore the roles these sources may play in performing various e-discovery tasks and discuss how the current relationships may change in the future.

Internal Expenditures

Though we took steps to help participating companies describe the extent to which internal resources, such as law department counsel and IT department staff members, played a role in the e-discovery production cycle, we were frequently told that the organization's employees' contributions to the process were "negligible" or "minor." The cases identified in this way were generally ones in which outside vendors were used for collection-related tasks, presumably because the organization lacked the capability to collect ESI in a forensically sound and defensible manner, because it was felt that vendor services would be more cost-effective or efficient than using in-house resources, or because the use of a vendor would provide for more-persuasive testimony about the collection process should it be questioned subsequently. We believe that, even in such situations, organizations would be undervaluing the efforts expended by in-house counsel and technology-support staff, efforts that might have consisted of little more than acting in a supervisory or liaison capacity between the organization and the selected collection vendors but nevertheless should be included in a measure of total e-discovery spend. Based on our discussions with the representatives of participating companies, it is unlikely that there would ever be a situation in which absolutely *no* time was spent by organizational employees in responding to a request for production of the organizations' own electronic documents and data, even if the key steps of collection, processing, and review were actually performed and managed by outside counsel or vendors.

Such an assumption is supported by evidence that organizational litigants are taking greater direct control over aspects of their own discovery productions.[1] For example, an informal canvassing of 276 corporate counsel in the United States in 2009 suggested that about half of the companies represented have performed at least some of the tasks required for the production of ESI in response to discovery requests, tasks that traditionally have been under

[1] According to the Association of Corporate Counsel, 2007, "Gone are the days when in-house counsel send out major projects to outside counsel, pay vague bills 'for services rendered,' and remain uninvolved while outside counsel determine what is necessary. . . ."

the control of outside counsel.[2] Though fees paid to law firms and vendors may continue to dominate the total spend for the foreseeable future, there is little question that many litigants are increasingly responsible for at least some portion of the costs and effort associated with pretrial discovery through direct expenditures of internal staff time, purchasing and implementation of discovery-related technology and hardware, and managing contracts with third-party vendors and consultants.[3] At a minimum, in-house counsel (or perhaps company paralegals or IT personnel) would spend at least some time assisting in the coordination of e-discovery tasks involving their companies' own information systems.

In order to account for possible underreporting of internal expenditures, we adjusted reported values slightly to prevent zero values for the contributions of company personnel. The adjustment is a very conservative one, essentially adding in a small amount of time for in-house counsel and IT support working in an ancillary capacity to the main work performed in the production process. We roughly estimated what two weeks of services from one law department attorney and one IT department technical-support member would "cost" the organization, initially using BLS *Occupational Employment Statistics* mean annual wage estimates for lawyers and network and computer system administrators in North American Industry Classification System (NAICS) Sector 55 (management of companies and enterprises).[4] The wage estimates were then used as the basis for calculating total compensation for these staff members, using BLS *Employer Costs for Employee Compensation* tables for the "Management, Professional, and Related" private industry occupation group.[5] Rounding the result to the nearest $1,000, we estimate that such services would require a total of $13,000 in compensation for the two positions over a two-week period.

Notwithstanding the addition of $13,000 to existing amounts for internal expenditures, such costs remain a fairly minor portion of the total. Three-quarters of the 41 cases for which we have data on this aspect have adjusted internal costs of less than 10 percent (see Figure 3.1).[6] There were some cases in which internal costs were 25 percent or more, but those were generally instances in which total expenditures were relatively modest, between $30,000 and $150,000.

Vendor Expenditures

In order to provide consistency in the manner in which we examine expenditures by source (i.e., internal, vendors, and outside counsel), we continue to assume an additional $13,000 in internal costs beyond those reported to us (so $13,000 would be added to the total e-discovery production spend). As can be seen in Figure 3.2, about three-fourths of the 41 cases with

---

[2] Fulbright and Jaworski, 2009, p. 59.

[3] The president of an in-house counsel bar association explained,

> The primary driver of legal costs is outside legal spending, which is roughly double the spending on in-house counsel; however, during the past several years the ratio has shifted in favor of law departments, reflecting more legal work being done in-house. (Association of Corporate Counsel, 2007)

[4] BLS, 2011b. The annual wage estimates for lawyers and network/system administrators were $158,340 and $73,630, respectively.

[5] BLS, 2011a. For this group, wages and salaries were reported to make up 70.8 percent of total compensation, while total benefits were 20.2 percent.

[6] See also Table A.7 in Appendix A.

Figure 3.1
Distribution of Cases by Percentage of Total Costs Consumed by Internal Expenditures, $13,000 Added to All Reported Internal Expenditures, 41 Cases

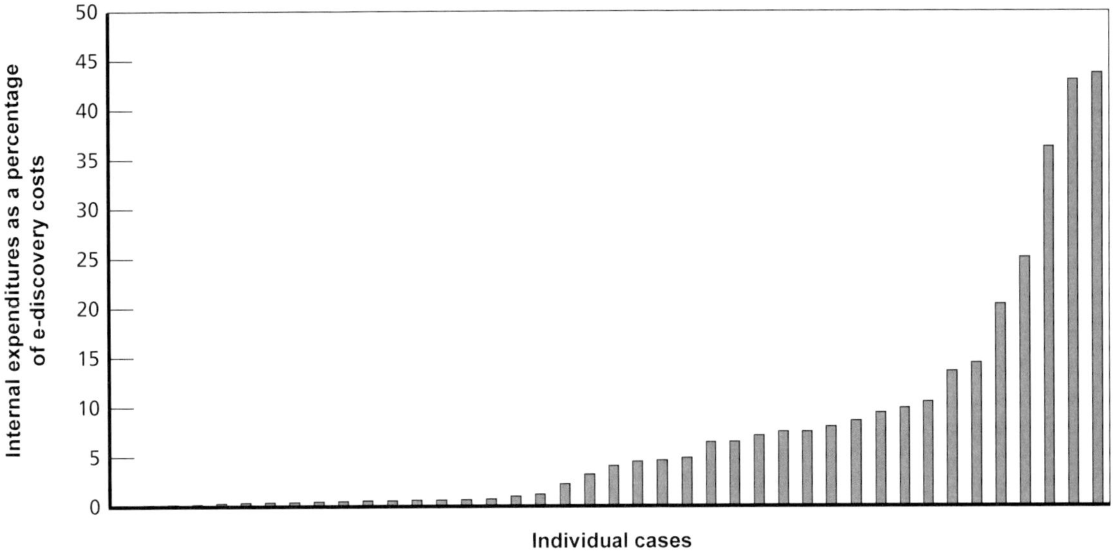

RAND *MG1208-3.1*

Figure 3.2
Distribution of Cases by Percentage of Total Costs Consumed by Vendor Expenditures, $13,000 Added to All Reported Internal Expenditures, 41 Cases

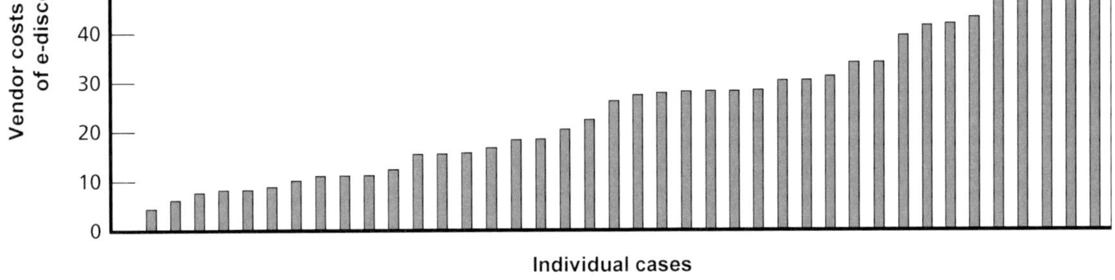

RAND *MG1208-3.2*

usable information in this regard reported that the proportion of vendor-related costs were between 11 percent and 34 percent, with a median of 26 percent.[7]

---

[7] See Table A.8 in Appendix A.

Outside Counsel Expenditures

Even including the adjustment we made to internal expenditures, outside counsel expenditures continue to make up the overwhelming majority of e-discovery costs in most of our sample cases. As shown in Figure 3.3, three-quarters of the 41 cases with usable information had outside counsel fees and expenses constituting 53 percent or more of the total spend, half were at 72 percent or more, and one-quarter were at 84 percent or more.[8]

Traditionally, when civil justice researchers have looked at the costs of litigation, a commonly employed assumption has been that outside counsel fees and expenses constituted all or nearly all of a litigant's legal transaction costs, suggesting that "legal fees" could be used "as a reasonable proxy for total monetary cost."[9] Counsel costs do appear to represent the bulk of expenditures for e-discovery production overall, but it is clear that there are cases in which counsel costs represented less than half of total spend. In three of the 41 cases we examined, essentially all e-discovery tasks were handled by the organizational litigant or vendors under its control. As such, future research into litigation costs will have to acknowledge the need to include in the analysis the monetary value of litigant time, as well as sometimes-significant ancillary expenses, such as those for vendor services.

Interestingly, our contact at one of the participating companies suggested that, when the demands for ESI arise out of regulatory investigations and other administrative actions, outside counsel has little to do other than the review. Table A.9 in Appendix A illustrates that, in fact, government subpoena–related cases have some of the lowest percentages for outside counsel services for document production. But, in e-discovery generally, the interests of in-house

Figure 3.3
Distribution of Cases by Percentage of Total Costs Consumed by Outside Counsel Expenditures, $13,000 Added to All Reported Internal Expenditures, 41 Cases

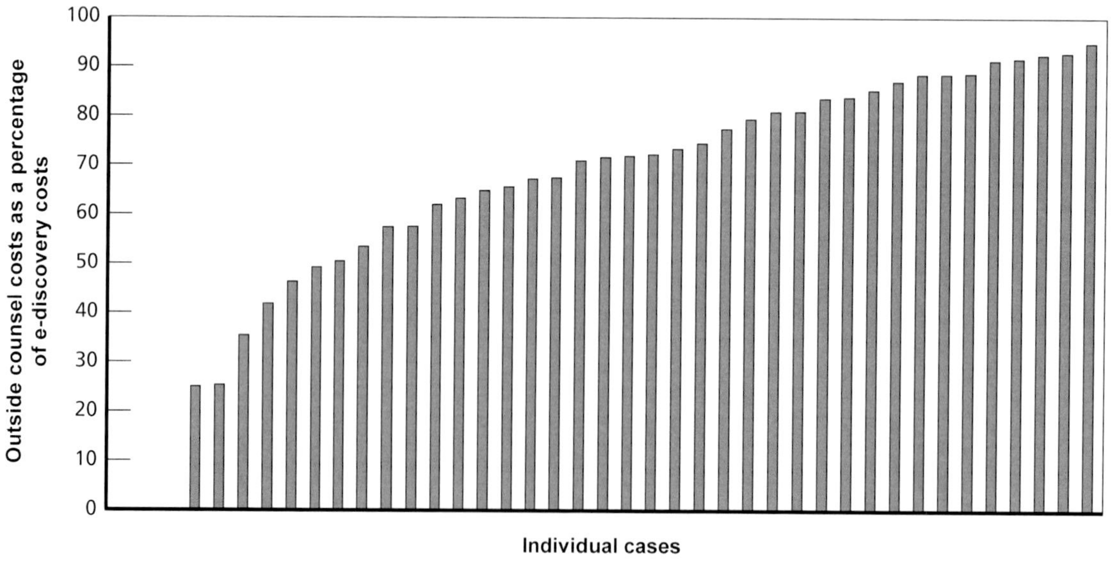

RAND *MG1208-3.3*

[8] See also Table A.9 in Appendix A.

[9] Trubek et al., 1983, p. 92.

counsel and their external law firm colleagues may not always be in precise alignment, with the potential for billing opportunities for review resulting in the law firms, at least according to one in-house contact, viewing the company's litigation demands as lucrative "cash cows," with each new e-discovery demand seen as "a bird's nest on the ground." It was asserted that, without close supervision of outside counsel's discovery-related decisions, "the whole thing can become a runaway train wreck."

Primary Sources for Different Production Phases

At least for the cases included in our sample, vendors play the largest role in collection and processing, while review is largely the domain of outside counsel (see Table 3.1). We have usable data for the source of collection expenditures for 42 cases. In 31 of those cases, the costs for vendor services exceeded those for either internal resources or outside counsel. Expenditures for vendors in the context of processing tasks were nearly always (42 of 44 cases) more than what was reported for other sources. It should be noted that the zero counts for internal processing do not mean that corporate resources were not consumed for processing, only that none of the cases reporting complete information had internal expenditures for such activities greater than its expenditures for external entities, such as vendors or outside counsel. In addition, two participating companies had brought many processing tasks in-house, and it is likely that additional cases in our study would have fallen into the "internal" cell for processing had data limitations regarding other aspects of the discovery process not prevented some of their cases from being included in Table 3.1. Outside counsel took the lead in handling review tasks in 45 of 59 cases, with vendors (such as offshore reviewers directly controlled by the corporate legal department) accounting for the other four cases.

It should also be noted that the case counts in Table 3.1 were not adjusted for potentially missing information regarding internal resource expenditures. Although we believe that it is most helpful to examine the relative contribution of the three key sources (internal resources, vendor services, and outside counsel representation) after a minor increase for internal expenditures is included, presenting the results contained in Table 3.1 in a similar way would require allocating the adjustment value across collection, processing, and review in some defensible way. Although we strongly suspect that internal corporate contributions to the e-discovery process are routinely underestimated, it is not possible to comfortably generalize about what tasks such organizational resources actually performed.[10]

[10] We did test applying the $13,000 adjustment to the internal resource expenditures in cases in our data under three scenarios: (1) all to collection expenses, (2) all to processing expenses, and (3) all to review expenses. The results do not meaningfully change with such adjustments; most cases in our data continue to report vendor expenses related to collection or processing exceeding those for internal resources or outside counsel and continue to report outside counsel expenses related to review exceeding those for vendors or internal resources. The one significant difference was that the number of cases in which the majority of collection expenses were for internal resources increased from six to 13, with a corresponding drop in cases in which vendor services predominated from 31 to 24 cases. But, even under such a scenario, vendors remained the top category of expenditure for collections in just more than half of the cases.

Table 3.1
Case Counts by the Primary Source of Expenditures for E-Discovery Tasks

Task	Internal	Vendor	Outside Counsel	Total Cases Reporting
Collection	6	31	5	42
Processing	0	42	2	44
Review	0	4	45	49

Future Trends

What did seem clear from our discussions is that the distribution of e-discovery tasks across internal resources, vendors, and outside counsel, as represented in Table 3.1, is likely to change in the near future. One company's representative summed up the attitude of many of our interviewees when he indicated that his company's future model will be to "double down" on the e-discovery tasks that it does best, try to insource as much of those tasks as possible, and then outsource everything else that can be "commoditized." Another company outlined its evolving philosophy as one in which "bringing the outside work inside and handling it with enterprise-class processes is the best approach." Collections are a good example of this likely trend, with discussions with our participating companies suggesting that the frequency in which organizational litigants take a primary role in conducting their own discovery data collection is on the rise. Two of the eight companies were in the process of implementing an automated, cross-network collection tool, and others were in the early planning stages. The results shown in Table 3.1 might therefore have differed had cases concluded in 2011 or 2012 been included.

Table 3.1 does suggest that, at least at the present time, vendors are the preferred choice for handling processing and hosting. One very large organization explained that, despite its considerable revenues and positive technological reputation within its own industry, it continued to lack any in-house capability to search through data, deduplicate, host for online review, preserve metadata, or produce in whatever form is required. But another company representative expressed considerable displeasure with that company's current approach of allowing outside counsel to choose the vendor for processing services. In that representative's experience, counsel-selected vendors simply do not do a good enough job of culling and other data-reduction tasks, choosing instead to convert larger-than-necessary amounts of data into image files and then send the product to outside counsel for an expensive, eyes-on review. This view was echoed to some degree by another participant, who indicated feeling that having a law firm handle most of the key production decisions and arrangements is not the most cost-effective approach. Although preferring to work collaboratively with outside law firms, that company now has its own set of preferred vendors for different parts of the process and different types of engagements. As was true for collection, the situation is somewhat in flux because some of the participating companies reported that they were in the middle of bringing some key processing tasks in-house, in part because of expanded capabilities of new collection tools (such as deduplication features) that they had or intended to purchase in the near future.

It is important to keep in mind that Table 3.1 reports only on the basis of estimated expenditures, not the number of hours of effort involved. For example, some cases that had been reported to us as having the bulk of their review costs arising from the services provided by outside counsel had actually had vendors perform a first-pass review on a much larger volume of data than was provided to the external law firm. Unlike what we were told about collection and processing, there does not seem to be a wholesale movement toward bringing the review process in-house, at least not insofar as having permanent employees of the organizational litigant take on more of the review for relevance, responsiveness, or privilege. What does seem likely is that legal departments, at least in the companies with whose representatives we spoke, will take greater control over how the first-pass review will be conducted, choosing vendors and specialized legal service law firms to perform functions formally within the purview of traditional outside counsel. Increased use of contract attorneys *directly* controlled by the organizational litigant does not seem to be the most attractive option, however; indeed, one participating company has significantly scaled back the core of contract attorneys that it maintains in-house, choosing instead to rely mostly on less expensive vendors for first-pass review. Some contacts, it should also be noted, reported that recent economic conditions had resulted in significant changes in their financial relationships with outside counsel. Pressure to reduce costs was said to have led to alternative billing arrangements and increased use by law firms of less expensive resources (such as contract attorneys and vendors) for review tasks. These developments were unlikely to have taken place during the discovery phases of most of the cases in our data collection. Internal resources may play a somewhat different role in the review process as well, even if the task continues to be left to the discretion of outside counsel or outsourced to vendors. In one participating company, the focus is now on permanently flagging data in its systems as privileged or not privileged whenever the data have been fully reviewed by outside counsel, by vendors, or by the law department. In this way, data deemed relevant and responsive (by whatever means) in an instant case will not require a new privilege review if those data have already been put through the process previously. The company reported that there were significant technological challenges to flagging documents in this way but that the effort needed to implement such a system was felt to be justified by potential cost savings.

CHAPTER FOUR

Reducing the Cost of Traditional Eyes-On Review

In this chapter, we describe two possibilities for reducing the costs of traditional review practices—reducing the cost of labor and increasing the speed at which lawyers can review documents—and we estimate the maximum savings that can be achieved through these means. We conclude the chapter by addressing the quality of review conducted by attorneys, which is currently considered the gold standard for assessing relevance, responsiveness, and privilege.

Introduction

With more than half of our cases reporting that review consumed at least 70 percent of the total costs of document production, this single area, described by one participant in our study as the "black hole" of the entire process, is an obvious target for reducing e-discovery expenditures. Neither collection nor processing elicited interviewee complaints as strident as those directed toward review challenges and expenditures. If organizational litigants are to make significant reductions in their e-discovery production costs for large-scale efforts similar to those included in our data, it will have to come in the area of review.

What would constitute a "significant reduction"? Obviously, such a determination would be a subjective one. However, for the review component of electronic-information production to be perceived by lawyers and their clients as a tolerable inconvenience in most instances, *it would arguably have to involve expenses that are no more burdensome than either the collection or processing phase.* Because expenses reported in our data collection roughly suggest that review consumes about \$0.73 of every dollar spent on ESI production, while collection and processing consume about \$0.08 and \$0.19, respectively (Figure 4.1), *traditional review costs would have to be reduced by about three-quarters* in order to make it no more expensive than processing, the next most costly component of production in large-scale e-discovery. Choosing a 75-percent reduction in review expenditures as the desired target is an admittedly arbitrary decision, but more-modest cost savings are not likely to end criticisms from some quarters that the advent of e-discovery has caused an unacceptable increase in the costs of resolving large-scale disputes.

Are such dramatic savings possible? Answering that question requires consideration of the two key components of review: the volume of information and the types of reviewers. Some participants in this study reported that review costs were relatively predictable at the point at which collected information has been processed. They claimed to have a good sense of how much money a review would require (absent unforeseen problems) based on the number of megabytes or document pages that are ready for review, once they decided on the final mix of law firms, vendors, in-house counsel, or contract attorneys who would be used. The complex-

Figure 4.1
Relative Costs of Producing Electronic Documents, by Task and by Source

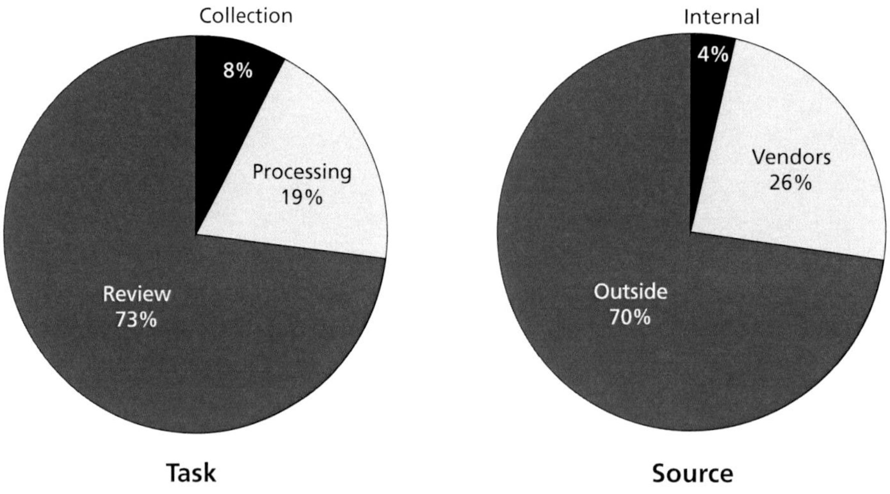

NOTE: Values reflect median percentages for cases with complete data, adjusted to 100 percent.
RAND *MG1208-4.1*

ity of the documents and specific needs of the case undoubtedly play a role in driving costs as well, but large-scale review is a process that has become commoditized, at least for the participants in our data collection. Figure 4.2 shows the relationship between the volume of reviewable documents and the total costs of the review. Though there are obvious exceptions in the distribution (and it should be noted that the data points in Figure 4.2 reflect a wide variety of approaches used to deal with review needs), the relationship between final costs and ESI volume is essentially a directly proportional one ($14,000 per gigabyte reviewed would be a good guideline here for most cases), with some decrease in the costs per gigabyte to review as volume increases.[1]

The cases represented in Figure 4.2 involved what might be thought of as *traditional* or *linear* reviews, in which attorneys are tasked with the job of looking at a document; making a decision about whether it is relevant, responsive, or privileged; and then moving to the next document in the queue. Often, the same group of attorneys handled all aspects of the review, but there were variations in approach. In some instances, the process was divided into distinct phases, with one team of reviewers examining the documents for relevance and responsiveness and a second team interested only in the privilege aspects of documents that had been flagged as relevant and responsive. In others, the set of documents was divided into various groups by subject matter or other criteria, with each group reviewed by a different law firm. But no matter how the process was structured, there was still a visual inspection of each document—in other words, an *eyes-on review.*

What we observed in our sample cases appears to be somewhat on the low side compared with publicly available review estimates by vendors, attorneys, and others for similar volumes of ESI. Table 4.1 presents some published estimates for the costs of reviewing ESI. Depend-

---

1 Figure 4.2 excludes the three cases with the greatest review volume in order to better present the relationship between volume and total review costs.

Figure 4.2
How the Volume of Data Reviewed Is Related to the Total Costs of Review, Largest-Volume Cases Excluded, 33 Cases

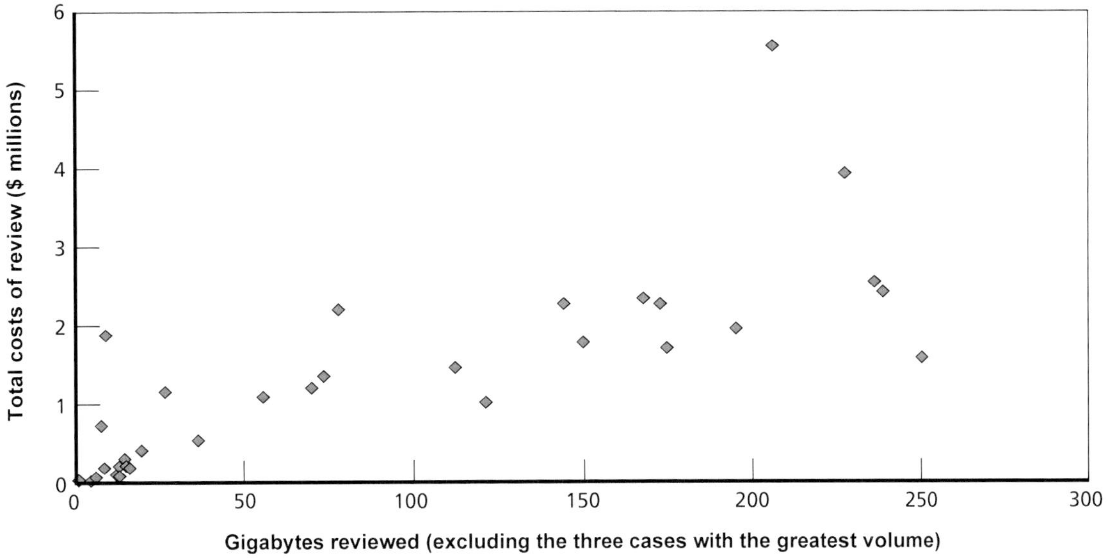

RAND *MG1208-4.2*

ing on the assumptions used for the hourly rates of reviewing counsel, the predicted productivity in the review process in terms of the average number of documents (or pages or bytes) examined per hour, and the average number of documents or pages in each gigabyte of data to be reviewed, estimates for pricing out this task range from $6,000 to $64,000 for every 10,000 documents examined.[2] Because the overall size of the set of reviewable documents is a function of the collection and processing stages, Table 4.1 suggests that, if the costs of eyes-on review are to be reduced to a level similar to those incurred for processing, there would have to be significant reductions in the current per-hour charges for attorneys or significant increases in the average volume of ESI that can currently be reviewed each hour. In the discussion that follows, we explore whether it is realistic to expect that such changes in the legal landscape can take place.

What Can Be Done About Attorney Rates?

As Table 4.1 suggests, there is great variation in the hourly rate charged by different types of attorneys. Although one reported national average for U.S. lawyers was $284 per hour in 2009, experience, location, firm size, and position in the firm all play a role in setting the market for billing rates.[3] One description of "typical" hourly rates for those involved in e-discovery reports that senior law firm partners bill at $450 per hour, junior partners at $350 per hour, associates

---

[2] One commonly employed assumption is that 10,000 documents is the equivalent of about 1 GB of data. But see Tredennick, 2011.

[3] "How, and How Much, Do Lawyers Charge?" undated, reporting the results of Incisive Legal Intelligence's *2009 Billing Rates and Practices Survey Report* of attorneys in small and mid-sized firms.

Table 4.1
Examples of Review Cost Estimates

Source	Volume and Productivity Assumptions	Reviewer Rate Assumptions ($ per hour)	Review Costs
Carlson, 2006	87.5 documents reviewed per hour	50	$5,714/10,000 documents
Deutchman, 2007	7,800 documents per gigabyte, 100 documents reviewed per hour	75	$5,850/GB, $7,500/10,000 documents
Austin, 2011	18,750 documents per gigabyte, 50 documents reviewed per hour	50	$18,750/GB, $10,000/10,000 documents
Paul and Baron, 2007	50 emails (and attachments) reviewed per hour	100	$20,000/10,000 emails
Sedona Conference, 2007	8,000 documents per gigabyte, 50 documents reviewed per hour	200	$32,000/GB, $40,000/10,000 documents
Skamser, 2008	75,000 pages per gigabyte, 300 pages reviewed per hour	Offshore: 40; onshore: 150	$10,000/GB (offshore) to $37,500/GB (onshore)
Egan and Homer, 2008	10,000 documents per gigabyte, 50 ("linear review") to 200 ("conceptual review") documents reviewed per hour	Offshore vendor: 28; contract attorney: 65; outside counsel: 200	$1,400/GB (conceptual review with offshore vendor, $1,400/10,000 documents) to $40,000/GB (linear review with outside counsel, $40,000/10,000 documents)
Clearwell Systems, 2010	50–75 documents reviewed per hour	200–300	$26,667/10,000 documents (high review rate at low hourly fee) to $60,000/10,000 documents (low review rate at high hourly fee)
Ruckman, 2008	31.25 documents reviewed per hour	200	$64,000/10,000 documents

NOTE: Review costs per gigabyte or 10,000 documents have been interpreted from the discussion in the source document. References to "document decisions per hour" have been treated as the equivalent of documents reviewed per hour. The table does not include costs of hosting for review if those were described in the source document. Reviewer rate assumptions reflect the amounts paid by the litigant, not the wages earned by the reviewer.

at $250 per hour, paralegals at $150 per hour, and contract attorneys at $75 per hour.[4] It should be kept in mind that these are rates billed to clients, not what the staff members actually earn.

Although there may well be instances in which partners, senior or otherwise, are used for document review, we assume that this happens in rare situations involving very small volumes of documents requiring especially sophisticated legal analysis or involving highly sensitive information. But even "ordinary" associates can bill out at rates of more than $200 per hour, and law firms have, on occasion, sought reimbursement at only slightly less expensive

[4] Vecella, Fasone, and Clark, 2009, p. 95.

rates for discovery-related services performed by their paralegals.[5] It is not likely, however, that clients will continue to accept the notion that paralegals or newly hired associates assigned to routine discovery tasks should bill their services at the same rates used for their trial appearances or appellate-brief writing. For example, one of our participants reported that a law firm used only infrequently had attempted to bill the company $350 per hour for review services provided by a junior associate; perhaps not surprisingly, the firm no longer receives any of the company's e-discovery business. Because organizational litigants are increasingly resistant to quietly acquiescing to whatever decisions their outside counsel make regarding review, law firms are offering deeply discounted services to their cost-conscious clients, and vendors are providing new alternatives to traditional hired counsel. The main approaches employed today consist of using contract attorneys, domestic legal process outsourcers, or foreign attorneys to conduct review.

Contract Attorneys and Domestic Legal Process Outsourcing

Contract attorneys have become a popular way to cut review costs, earning hourly wages greater than those for a law firm's full-time paralegals but without the additional costs of providing benefits and other forms of compensation. A law firm might, for example, directly hire relatively inexpensive lawyers to work on specific projects or for a specific period of time. Alternatively, the firm might bring in temporary attorneys who are located, hired, and paid by legal staffing agencies. Either approach creates a third tier of lawyers within a firm, ones who would not be on the same partnership track as associates and who could be paid a much lower salary with reduced benefits, or perhaps no benefits at all. Another involves the use of legal process outsourcing (LPO) companies operating in the United States that have the ability to quickly ramp up for large-scale reviews using either temporary lawyers they hire on a project basis or permanent staff attorneys who are presumably being paid about the same as temporary hires at traditional law firms. Note that the hourly wages paid to the contract attorneys or domestic LPO employees, the per-hour fees paid by law firms to LPOs for their services or to legal staffing agencies for providing temporary attorneys, and the hourly rates actually charged to litigants may all be quite different. So costs for eyes-on review using alternatives, such as contract attorneys or domestic LPOs, may be 25–75 percent less than what might be thought of as the traditional approach, in which junior associates are used for such work.

There are risks that must be considered when using contract attorneys or domestic LPOs. Despite approval of the general practice by the ABA, ethical questions can arise from the use of temporary counsel or third-party providers of attorney services, including difficulties regarding potential conflicts of interest, potential waivers of the attorney-client privilege, client disclosure, informed consent to the use of nonstaff attorneys, and justifying the difference between what the contract attorneys or LPOs charge and what is actually billed to the clients.[6] Presumably, large, sophisticated organizational litigants are fully aware of such risks and would much prefer taking them than paying double, triple, or more for traditional law firm document-review services. It should be noted that the use of contract attorneys and LPOs does not elimi-

---

[5] See, e.g., *Zubulake v. UBS Warburg LLC*, 216 F.R.D. 280 (S.D.N.Y. 2003) (litigant incurred costs of $170 per hour for its law firm's paralegals, though the judge in the case noted that paralegal services could be obtained "for far less"); and *Lucky Brand Dungarees, Inc. v. Ally Apparel Res. LLC*, 2009 WL 466136 (S.D.N.Y. Feb. 25, 2009) (approving rate requests of $205–235 per hour for paralegals).

[6] See, e.g., ABA Formal Op. 88-356 (1988) and ABA Formal Op. 08-451 (2008).

nate the need for attorneys closely connected to the case to be involved in the review process. In-house or outside counsel would still have an ethical obligation to manage review activities and supervise the work being conducted on the litigant's behalf.[7]

It is not clear, however, whether litigants can count on any future decline in what they must spend for review services using attorneys licensed in the United States, even for those offering their services on a contract basis. Recent economic woes, along with rising numbers of law school graduates, have indeed produced a glut of attorneys, many of whom have found themselves in a situation in which contracted review has become one of the few viable options for maintaining a steady income stream.[8] Arguably one of the least glamorous segments of the legal services industry, the use of large numbers of temporary licensed attorneys to perform eyes-on review has blossomed in recent years, with what appears to be a corresponding increase in complaints about pay and working conditions voiced by practitioners who take such positions.[9] In New York City, a location known for relatively high costs of living, licensed attorneys working on a contract basis in a large-scale review operation might receive no more than $25 per hour without benefits, be expected to review 80 to 100 documents per hour, have no expectations that the position will last more than a few weeks or months (early terminations of review projects due to settlement are frequent occurrences), and are sometimes required to work in excess of 12 hours per day without overtime pay.[10] Although the apparent oversupply of attorneys is likely to last for some time, it is not realistic to expect that hourly rates will continue to plunge indefinitely.[11] Even if high-volume document-review projects migrate to areas of the country where wages are more modest (compensation for review attorneys can be $15 or less per hour outside major metropolitan areas), there may not be much additional room for cutting wages.[12] Recent law school graduates, who fill many review positions, often incur significant debt arising from tuition, sometimes in excess of $100,000, creating what amounts to a virtual floor for the hourly wages paid to even the most cash-strapped American attorney.[13]

---

[7] ABA Formal Op. 08-451 (2008) (lawyers must "ensure that tasks are delegated to individuals who are competent to perform them, and then to oversee the execution of the project adequately and appropriately").

[8] Rampell, 2011 ("across the country, there were twice as many people who passed the bar in 2009 [53,508] as there were openings [26,239]"); Clay and Seeger, 2010 ("When asked about other staffing alternatives, firms expressed a growing enthusiasm for contract lawyers").

[9] See, e.g., O'Connell, 2011a, p. B1; Greenwood, 2007.

[10] For examples of recent postings for temporary document-review positions in New York City, see helpme123, undated. See also O'Connell, 2011a, p. B1. It should be noted that $25 per hour appears to be at the lower end of the range for document-review attorneys in the New York metropolitan area ($30–35 is perhaps a more frequently mentioned rate).

[11] Indeed, there are indications that some cost savings currently enjoyed by those who employ contract attorneys may be at risk. The practice of denying overtime pay for workdays exceeding eight hours has been the subject of a legal challenge. See O'Connell, 2011b, p. B2. The use of contract attorneys without regard to where they are licensed has been curtailed in at least one jurisdiction (see Schwartz, 2005).

[12] For example, job listings posted on the Massachusetts School of Law at Andover website offered document-review positions paying $12 per hour in Attleboro, Massachusetts, and $15 per hour in Wheeling, West Virginia (copy on file with the authors).

[13] ABA, 2009a, states,

> When one adds books and living expenses to tuition, the average public law student borrows $71,436 for law school, while the average private school student borrows $91,506. Many students borrow far more than $100,000, and these numbers do not even include debt that students may still carry from their undergraduate years.

Foreign Attorneys

One reason that U.S. contract attorneys are paid such relatively modest hourly rates for review (at least compared with their law firm associate counterparts) is that they now face serious competition from lawyers located in other countries. Some LPOs operate facilities in such countries as India or the Philippines, to take advantage of a large supply of locally licensed attorneys who speak and understand English and who would presumably work for much less than U.S.-barred counsel. It has been reported that junior attorneys in India at such "offshore LPOs" can make about $8,200 per year, a substantial discount from the $77,000 that one organization estimates to be the average starting salary earned by recent U.S. law school graduates in full-time jobs and even compared with the $52,000 that would be paid over the course of a year to a contract attorney receiving $25 per hour.[14] It may be misleading to directly compare the wages earned by contract attorneys in the United States with those earned by members of the bar in other countries because the real concern to organizational litigants is not the relative salaries of the reviewers but the total costs per hour (or per document, or per page, or per gigabyte) they must ultimately pay for review services. Such expenditures reflect not only the reviewer's wages but also the markup imposed on those services by LPOs or outside law firms for managing the review process, attorney training, quality control, review platform implementation, various overhead expenses, and making a profit. Many of these cost factors also apply to instances in which the offshore attorneys work for "captive centers" maintained by large organizational litigants themselves that seek to bypass intermediaries, such as LPOs, or have greater control over their corporate documents and data. In addition, many offshore review offerings are bundled with other e-discovery services or are priced by the unit rather than the reviewer-hour, which can make providing comparable figures somewhat difficult. Nevertheless, there are reports that some offshore LPOs charge $10–25 per hour for "low-end work" (presumably the type of services that would include first-pass document review), with other published examples of offshore rates in about the same general range.[15] This represents a substantial savings over U.S. contract attorneys managed by law firms, which might bill out those services at rates two,[16] four,[17] six,[18] or ten times[19] what the attorneys were actually paid. Presumably, the markup would be less when the review is conducted by domestic LPOs offering commoditized review services by U.S. attorneys. But even though organizational litigants that routinely employ contract attorneys in the United States directly would have total expenditures even closer to the actual salaries paid to the temporary lawyers, their per-hour costs for review services are still likely to be much more than those charged by offshore LPOs.

One estimate often used for the minimum annual salary required to "break even" given the investment required to go to law school is $65,315 (ABA, 2009a). Assuming a 40-hour week and a 52-week year, this would require about $31 per hour in compensation, which would be at the high end of the scale for contract review. Other estimates of the break-even point are higher. See, e.g., Schlunk, 2009.

[14] Cotts and Kufchock, 2007; National Association for Law Placement, 2011. Assuming 40 hours of work each week for 52 continuous weeks.

[15] Cotts and Kufchock, 2007; see also, e.g., Egan and Homer, 2008 ($28 per hour); Stevens, 2011 ($15–20 per hour).

[16] Schwartz, 2005.

[17] "Down in the Data Mines," 2008.

[18] Malan, 2009.

[19] O'Connell, 2011b.

Have offshore review fees bottomed out, as we suggest has happened with domestic contract attorney services? Given that there are few technical restrictions on where offshore LPOs might be located in an increasingly networked world and only limited legal environment requirements imposed by U.S. professional organizations,[20] expansion beyond the current concentration of offshore review services in India (and, to a lesser extent, the Philippines) is likely. Some vendor advertising touts the advantages of review facilities located in common-law countries where English is the predominant language. However, there are few insurmountable systemic or language barriers to opening up operations in just about any relatively stable nation with an appropriate level of respect for the rule of law. Indeed, the Philippine legal system was based on Spanish civil law, and only about one in nine Indians uses English as a first or second language. China, Sri Lanka, Argentina, and South Korea have all been mentioned as other possibilities for large-scale offshore LPO operations. With a seemingly unlimited global pool of reviewers potentially available to handle review duties for a fraction of the costs of even temporary contract attorneys in the United States, there is a reasonable potential that even the $10-per-hour rate reported for low-cost offshore review will fall in the future.

But despite the obvious attraction of lower review costs, concerns have been voiced about using foreign attorneys for legal services, specifically ones who have not been admitted to the bar in any U.S. jurisdiction. One involves the inapplicability of ethical rules developed to regulate the legal profession in the 50 states and the District of Columbia, most notably in regard to confidentiality protections and conflicts of interest.[21] Rather than relying on an existing umbrella of ethical rules in the United States to protect clients in case of error or intentional misconduct, similar safeguards can only be contractually imposed on LPOs and their attorneys, leaving enforcement and relief up to foreign courts and judges. Checking for conflicts of interest can be problematic when offshore LPOs sell services to a wide variety of clients, or when local attorneys move from one operation to another. Review of materials involving certain types of intellectual property can result in the disclosure of sensitive technology to non-U.S. citizens, which may run afoul of International Traffic in Arms Regulations and Export Administration Regulations. Another concern has been about the way reviewers might interpret U.S. English colloquialisms and cultural references, a potential problem when emails and other informal communications are the primary subjects of the document review. Information security breaches are also oft-mentioned risks of using offshore LPOs, as are inadequate professional liability insurance, the lack of in-country regulatory oversight, and possible problems with maintaining the work-product privilege. Though there are no insurmountable ethical hurdles to using offshore LPOs, a key requirement is that a U.S.-licensed attorney exercise "direct supervisory authority" over the lawyers performing the services.[22] But such supervision may be made more difficult not only because of distances and cultural differences but also because of local regulation against the unlicensed practice of law by foreign (U.S., in this instance) attorneys ostensibly overseeing the review.[23] In response to such concerns, offshore

[20] For example, ABA Formal Opinion 08-451, 2008, suggests that any "lack of rigorous training or effective lawyer discipline does not mean that individuals from that nation cannot be engaged to work on a particular project," only that, under such circumstances, it would be "more important" for the outsourcing attorney to scrutinize the work.

[21] Barlyn, 2008.

[22] See ABA Formal Opinion 08-451, 2008.

[23] See, e.g., "Writ Petition Filed Against 31 Foreign Law Firms and an LPO," 2010.

LPOs argue that problems, such as information security and confidentiality, can be minimized through the imposition of various procedural and contractual safeguards and that continued evolution in the collaborative relationship between U.S. counsel and offshore providers will address supervisory issues.[24] Nevertheless, there may continue to be resistance to the idea of shifting most document-review operations to overseas providers, thus making offshore LPOs a viable solution for sophisticated organizations comfortable with sending sometimes-sensitive information to third-party vendors located in other countries, but not necessarily the answer for most litigants.[25]

Increasing Review Speed

The second key factor influencing the variation in review costs is the average volume (however measured) of data that can be reviewed by an attorney over a period of time (see Table 4.1). Although the approach, experience, and motivation of the attorney are of obvious importance, productivity is also closely linked to the nature of the data being reviewed, the goals of the review, and the process by which the review is conducted. For example, the rate for documents reviewed per hour is likely to be higher if most of what is to be reviewed comes in the form of one- or two-paragraph emails rather than multipage technical reports. Rates would also be affected by the review tool's features and general "user-friendliness"; whether coding for subject matter or other criteria were required as well; whether attachments would need to be routinely opened on examined documents; whether the documents viewed are already organized by topic or in some other way; whether the documents require a detailed reading or just a quick scan; whether additional information about the document would be available to the coder (such as the subject line of an email or the author); and whether the review was intended to be for privilege, for relevance and responsiveness, for sensitive information, for identifying hot documents, or for some combination of the above. Thus, reported review rates have to be viewed as extremely rough benchmarks only, because what is being reviewed and how it is to be accomplished can vary significantly from project to project.

In Table 4.1, reported review rates varied from 31 to 100 documents per hour for traditional review approaches, but it is not clear whether the sources for those values were really describing the same sort of effort. Nevertheless, other published estimates fall roughly in the same range (see Table 4.2).

---

[24] Ross, 2011.

[25] Another option for litigants and their counsel would be to dispense with using licensed attorneys for the review. The "review of documents for potential relevance or potential privilege" has been characterized as "work that seems to call for little or no application of legal knowledge, training or judgment," so it is not clear why lawyers must always be used if "the ultimate decision to assert the privilege and produce or not produce the document will be made by someone else" (D.C. Ct. App., *Compliance with Rule 49 by 'Contract' Lawyers in the District of Columbia*, Op. 16-05, June 17, 2005, p. 3). There is nothing revolutionary about such an approach because law office paralegals, secretaries, and interns have participated in many reviews. What would be a significant shift in traditional practices would be to have the *bulk* of large-scale reviews performed by nonlegal staff, such as college students or other temporary hires. Although there are no insurmountable ethical hurdles in this regard (see ABA Formal Opinion 08-451, 2008), our research suggests that the frequency with which nonlegal staff in the United States are used to perform reviews is trivial compared with the much more common employment of outside counsel, paralegals, contract attorneys, organizational litigant law department staff, domestic LPOs, and offshore LPOs for these purposes.

Table 4.2
Examples of Reported Rates of Traditional Review

Source	Rate
helpme123, 2009	"They are expecting you to do about 80 docs an hour. . . ."
Shah, undated	"assuming that a lawyer or paralegal can review 50 documents per hour (a very fast review rate)"
Epiq Systems, 2009	"As a general guideline, the average reviewer should be able to review 50 documents per hour." "The average rate of review in most projects is 30 documents per hour."
Egan and Homer, 2008	"For a typical linear review, an industry-recognized standard is approximately 50 documents per hour. . . ."
Court filing, 2011a	"In our experience, a typical document reviewer reviews approximately 60 documents per hour. . . ."
Dutton, 2010	"[R]espondents in this survey reported a mean of 84 and a median of 85 documents per reviewer per hour. . . ."

[a] Declaration of Caroline Boudreau Sweeney, filed July 15, 2011, *Brown v. Ameriprise Fin. Servs., Inc.*, Docket No. 0:09-cv-02413, D. Minn.

Despite likely differences in the assumptions underlying these estimates, each presumably reflecting different experiences with attorney types, incentives provided for maximizing output, and the nature of the data, the numbers suggest that there are shared expectations among vendors, litigants, and law firms about how many documents a person can actually be expected to review. The upper bound for reported rates approaches 100 documents per hour, which we assume involves reviewers with the strongest motivations and experience in this area, as well as documents simple enough that a decision on relevance, responsiveness, privilege, or confidential information could be made in an average of 36 seconds. Such a short period of time means that documents must be fairly brief, even under optimal conditions. A trained "speed reader," for example, can skim written materials at roughly 1,000 words per minute with about 50-percent comprehension,[26] so even allocating zero time for bringing up a new document on the screen, as well as zero time for contemplating a decision or the act of clicking the appropriate button to code a choice, the average number of words in the document could not exceed 600 when skimming at a very high rate. In a document with 250 words per page, 600 words fills about a page and a half of text. Given the trade-off between reading speed and comprehension, especially in light of the complexity of documents subject to discovery in large-scale litigation, it is unrealistic to expect much room for improvement in the rates of unassisted human linear review.

Grouping Documents to Speed Review

In recent years, there has been a concerted effort to rethink how review is conducted, with the goal of moving away from the current paradigm of a reviewer examining every document individually and in whatever order in which the documents fell following the processing phase. Borrowing from the field of semantic analysis, one commonly employed approach groups simi-

[26] Marks-Beale and Mullan, 2008, p. 112.

lar documents together, so that each "set" shares, for example, common themes, topics, passages, senders, receivers, dates, or other criteria.[27]

Two potential benefits are said to arise from this technique. First, reviewers can move through the corpus of documents more efficiently because a complete picture of an event, a conversation, a problem, an employee, a project, or whatever the grouping was based on would be available. With fewer "holes" in the story and additional context for what is presented on the review tool's screen, it would be easier (and presumably faster) to decide on issues, such as relevance or responsiveness. Second, under certain circumstances, the reviewer might need to examine only a single example from each set, and the decision on relevance, responsiveness, or privilege made on that document could be automatically applied to the others.

Three techniques are most commonly used for grouping documents in this fashion:

- *Near-duplicate detection.* This technique groups together documents that contain mostly identical blocks of text or other information while differing in some way (if two or more documents were, in fact, completely identical, all but one should have been dropped during the prior processing phase as part of deduplication efforts). Such differences can include minor amounts of additional or deleted text, altered formats, or variation in file types. One example of a near-duplicate would be a word processing document file and a scan of a printed version of that same document after being subjected to OCR. Another example of near-duplicates would be multiple drafts of the same document, with only slight differences between revisions. When grouped in this way, the reviewer might decide that, for example, because the "master" or "pivot" document in the set (the one that is judged to be most representative of the entire group) appears to be relevant and responsive, it is therefore not necessary to examine the other documents in the same set. Some applications highlight the differences between the master document and the related ones, thus allowing the reviewer to more quickly determine whether others in the group should be coded differently from the first viewed. Whether two documents are near-duplicates is essentially a subjective judgment, and applications allow users to adjust the *similarity threshold* (sometimes referred to as a *likeness threshold* or *resemblance threshold*), the statistical value that determines how close to an exact match the documents must be to be classified as a near-duplicate.
- *Clustering.* Sometimes referred to as *topic clustering* or *concept clustering*, this technique first identifies the *keywords* (often all the nouns, as well as lexical verbs that represent actions, events, and states) in each document. Documents can then be grouped by the degree to which they share such keywords, with greater similarity increasing the probability that the same topic is addressed in the text. The algorithms for calculating similarity depend on the application, as does the manner in which the process takes place. Some clustering tools create such groups automatically; others do so only after human decisions have been made about which keywords are of greatest interest and which can be ignored, while others use documents of known importance as the "seeds" for clusters of similar

[27] An argument can be made that, in many (or perhaps most) reviews, the documents already share many important commonalities. They may have been identified using the same keyword searches, come from the same custodians or data locations, or been created during the same span of time. The grouping described here is far more tightly connected and might involve, for example, just ten documents determined to satisfy a specific grouping criteria out of tens of thousands related to the same product.

files. Though clustering's primary benefit to the review process may be in the way it organizes documents by topic rather than in random order (thus streamlining the examination), there are tools that can identify a representative document from each cluster, giving the reviewer the option of applying a decision based on the representative document to the entire set.

- *Email threading.* When the set of emails subject to review has been threaded, reviewers are able to look at groups of messages involving similar conversations or discussions, with all forwards, replies, cc's, and bcc's listed in chronological order and essentially duplicate materials within the thread eliminated. The groupings can be based on the metadata (e.g., author, date, subject line, or recipient) or on the content of the message body. Grouping by the content in the body of the emails may involve techniques similar to content clustering or near-duplicate detection. Depending on the approach, the differences between the master or "parent" email and the "children" emails in the same set might be highlighted for the reviewer. Threading technology can also include the ability to view the emails within threads in various ways, such as by author or in reverse chronological order.[28]

Such techniques might be thought of as *leveraging analytics*, processes intended to enhance existing human reviewer productivity either through greater efficiency in the review or the ability to bulk-code like documents.[29] Commercial vendors touting the cost savings of near-duplicate detection, clustering, and threading, sometimes referred to as *similarity-detection technologies*, assert that effective review rates of 120, 150, 175, 250, 300–500, and even exceeding 1,000 documents per hour are indeed possible.[30] One must assume that, at the upper end of these rates, the greatest efficiencies are gained by the ability to bulk-code large blocks of documents in similar ways. Given the limits on how quickly people can read and comprehend written information, an effective review rate of many hundreds of documents per hour could be achieved only if the decisions reviewers make about individual documents can be applied to dozens or hundreds of essentially similar items.[31] Increased efficiency through better organization of the corpus of documents would not account for a fivefold increase in review rates.

The Potential for Cost Savings Through Leveraging Analytics

Near-Duplicate Detection. The key prerequisite for the use of all these techniques is that large numbers of documents must have a level of similarity that would be acceptable to counsel responsible for overseeing the review effort. Vendor estimates of the percentage of documents in reviews that may, in fact, be near-duplicates, for example, include ranges of 20–30 percent,

---

[28] Far from being the exclusive domain of sophisticated e-discovery vendors, a simple version of email threading is now found in consumer email platforms, such as Google Gmail and Microsoft Outlook 2010, which refer to organizing messages in this way as *conversation* views.

[29] These approaches should not be confused with the more–commonly utilized techniques intended to reduce review costs by reducing the volume of documents needing review (such as deduplication or more-refined keyword searches to cull already-collected data). With these techniques, a set of 1 million documents for review continues to consist of 1 million documents after the analytics have been applied, and some eyes-on review would still be very much in the equation.

[30] IBM, 2010; Iris Data Services, 2009; kCura, undated; Attenex, undated; Stratify, 2008. See also, e.g., Borden et al., 2011 ("1,131 documents per hour"); and IPRO Tech, undated ("rates up to 1,500 documents per hour"). For additional examples of effective review rates reportedly exceeding 100 documents per hour, see Borden, 2010, pp. 3–4.

[31] One would assume that best practice requires that quality-assurance steps be taken to confirm the reliability of such bulk-coding decisions, including the eyes-on inspection of samples of documents in large clusters.

25–50 percent, 30–50 percent, and 30–60 percent.[32] It is not clear, however, whether such numbers would be typical of most e-discovery reviews or whether these reports select only examples of successful vendor projects with unusually high concentrations of near-duplicate documents. Moreover, although the mathematics of calculating document similarity are well established, there is no uniform standard for how close documents must be to qualify as near-duplicates within the context of a legal environment, ones that can be safely categorized in terms of relevance, responsiveness, or privilege based on an examination of just one member of the same set.[33] Lowering that similarity threshold will identify additional documents as acceptably close to at least one other in content, producing fewer groupings but with larger numbers of like documents within each group, and ultimately increasing the cost savings that can be realized from bulk coding. For example, an examination of a publicly available data set often used for research studies and benchmarking in the area of e-discovery reported that setting the threshold at 75-percent similarity resulted in identifying 21 percent of the documents as near-duplicates. However, when the threshold was reduced to 50 percent, the near-duplicate percentage increased to 40 percent.[34] Such an adjustment means that fewer individual items will require inspection, but it also increases the risk that decisions based on a single master document may be incorrectly applied to other documents within the same set. This trade-off between minimizing review expenditures and maximizing confidence in bulk-coding decisions requires difficult choices by attorneys who are traditionally risk averse.

It is unlikely that near-duplicate detection would be the sole answer to the overwhelming costs of large-scale review. The technique does have the potential of reducing those costs by 30 percent (assuming a conservative threshold setting)—a welcome relief for litigants, to be sure, but not one that would drop review expenditures to the levels observed in the processing stage.

Clustering. The potential advantages of clustering are similar to near-duplicate detection: Clustering provides an opportunity for bulk coding and a better overview of the story being told by the data. Many of the benefits of clustering touted by vendors relate to enhancing the analysis of large bodies of documents for the purpose of understanding what they contain and identifying items of specific interest. Such capabilities are, no doubt, important for both producing and demanding parties to make sense of hundreds or thousands of gigabytes of data in their possession, but *review expenditures* are our primary concern here.

Gauging the potential impact of clustering on review costs is more problematic than near-duplicate detection or threading. As we have discussed, estimated percentages of reduction of information by identifying near-duplicates or threading emails have been determined empirically. But the number and size of concept clusters within a body of documents is completely driven by both the content of those documents and the specific choices made by the review

---

[32] Driver, 2007 (interviewing Warwick Sharp); Equivio, 2009b; HaystackID, 2011; Intelligent Discovery Management, undated.

[33] Landauer and Dumais, 1997. Thresholds of 75–80 percent may be a commonly employed value:

> Each legal team can specify the threshold value (most likely 75 percent) that controls the grouping of near-duplicate documents. Some technologies use a default threshold of 80% similarity for near-duplicate detection. For larger review teams, it may be beneficial to tune this number down somewhat to reduce the risk of similar documents being assigned across different review resources. Any value of less than 50% is not typically useful for review but could be of benefit in reporting on the scope of a document collection. (Childress, 2009)

[34] Equivio, undated, Table 1, p. 5.

managers about which topical keywords are of greatest importance to the litigation at hand or which example documents should be used as seeds for the clustering.[35] This may be part of the explanation for the dearth of details regarding efficiencies that have been realized from applying clustering techniques. There are numerous vendor claims, no doubt made in good faith, that clustering will save money when applied to documents requiring review, but whether those savings are 5 percent or 50 percent compared with an unclustered review is not obvious from the research literature or vendor advertising. It is also unclear whether such claims are based on clustering's assistance in bulk coding or on the manner in which documents are organized for review. As such, we assume that clustering may well have a significant downward influence on review costs in some cases, but not in others, and perhaps not in most e-discovery productions.

Email Threading. Because of the heavy concentration of emails in many document reviews, threading certainly has the potential for bringing increased efficiency to the process. The ability to look at conversations holistically would reduce any time now spent by reviewers to get up to speed on what email senders and receivers were discussing. But threading may not always be a way to slash review costs to the point at which they approach those for processing or collection. A 2009 survey of vendors offering threading services asked the providers for an estimate of the average cost savings that had been realized by their clients as a result of the technique.[36] The six vendors responding to the question reported an average of 36 percent in savings, but the wide range of responses provided (10, 20, 25, 30, 58, and 75 percent) suggests that the benefits of the approach are not very predictable, even for those who employ the strategy on a regular basis. A more transparent calculation of potential benefits of threading comes from an examination of the Enron email data set, a digital warehouse of emails sent and received by senior management personnel at the collapsed corporation and subsequently made available to the public by the Federal Energy Regulatory Commission.[37] It was estimated that 123,501 (62 percent) of 200,399 emails were part of 30,091 threads containing two or more messages.[38] Applying threading techniques to this set can be viewed as reducing the number of individual "items" that must be reviewed by about 47 percent (76,898 single emails plus 30,091 multiple-email threads). However, because a reviewer would presumably need to spend more time on the average threaded set of multiple emails than on the average individual email, the savings would be something less than the 47-percent figure would suggest. Indeed, 18 percent of the threads contained five or more individual emails, each of which might have to be examined to determine whether something of interest was present.[39] Though presumably the general subject matter might hold constant throughout the thread, the individual messages combined into one location are not near-duplicates that can be safely ignored as redundant. If other corporate email collections exhibit similar characteristics, email threading is not likely to result in the collapsing of overwhelming percentages of collected and processed data, at least

---

[35] Although there are approaches that cluster automatically (sometimes referred to as *dynamic clustering* or *unsupervised clustering*), a human will eventually be required to decide on the subset of commonly identified keywords that are of greatest interest.

[36] Kershaw and Howie, 2010a.

[37] See Cohen, 2009.

[38] Klimt and Yang, 2004, pp. 224–225.

[39] See, e.g., *Baxter Healthcare Corp. v. Fresenius Medical Care Holding, Inc.*, 2008 WL 4547190 (N.D. Cal., October 10, 2008) ("Each email is a separate communication, for which a privilege may or may not be applicable. Defendants cannot justify aggregating authors and recipients for all emails in a string and then claiming privilege for the aggregated emails").

not to the degree reported for grouping of near-duplicate documents. Threaded emails would appear to make the job of review easier, more efficient, and perhaps more accurate, but not necessarily faster on a scale that would significantly reduce the costs of review.

Accuracy of Traditional Review

Before we turn to cost-saving approaches that move beyond traditional review, it is important to assess the quality of eyes-on examination of documents as the benchmark to compare with possible alternatives. Just how accurate is the traditional approach in these days of computerized review tools flashing pages on screen before a first-year associate or contract lawyer at rates exceeding 50 documents per hour? Comments made by current and former review attorneys may be instructive:

> For more and more law school graduates, this is the legal life: On a given day, they may plow through a few hundred documents—e-mails, PowerPoint presentations, memos, and anything else on a hard drive. Each document appears on their computer screen. They read it, then click one of the buttons on the screen that says "relevant" or "not relevant," and then they look at the next document.[40]

> I'm also a former doc review attorney. I remember on my first project, the supervisor said "any document with 'x' word in it is relevant" (don't remember what the word was). So we literally sat there for 12 hours a day (minimum required), 7 days a week, looking for x word. And we had to make sure that we fully expanded native documents, like spreadsheets. Never mind that half the temps there didn't do it, so as it moved up the food chain, someone higher up would have to do what someone farther down didn't do. And somehow the temps became the final word on whether something was relevant or not (at the seventh review of the documents). I remember being told that and thinking, you seriously want me to be the final word on whether this document is relevant, even though my entire knowledge of this case is based on the 15 minute conversation you had with all the temps at the beginning of the project?? Is it any wonder that privileged information gets through time and again, when the people who *should* be the final arbiters are nowhere to be found? I think not.[41]

These accounts offer a stark contrast to the image of senior counsel thoughtfully and deliberately reading each of his or her client's documents and bringing to bear years of training and experience as a litigator to the task. But they reflect the new reality of review. The need to conduct review in a highly competitive market can place enormous pressure on litigants and law firms to reduce expenses at every opportunity; in many instances, that pressure is, in turn, transferred to contract attorneys and vendors to offer their services at the lowest rates possible with the highest output. Such an industrialization of the review process would be acceptable if, in fact, the decisions being made were reasonably accurate and able to be replicated by other attorneys of similar experience and familiarity with the subject matter of the litigation. But

[40] Greenwood, 2007.

[41] Ronnie, 2011.

there is a body of compelling empirical evidence suggesting that outcomes fall well short of such an ideal.

In what follows, we summarize the findings of studies as evidence that human reviewers often disagree when they review the same set of documents for relevance and responsiveness in large-scale reviews. In one study, a sample of 5,000 documents from an actual production were reviewed by two different teams (A and B) of experienced reviewers supplied by two legal review services vendors, each team tasked with determining whether the documents were responsive to the demand in the original matter.[42] The decisions from the two teams were then compared with those of the attorneys in the original review and with each other. Although some disagreement between decisionmakers is to be expected, the results suggest that traditional review approaches may not be as consistent in decisionmaking as commonly believed. The original reviewers judged 9.8 percent of the documents to be responsive, but the corresponding rates for teams A and B were 24.2 and 28.8 percent, respectively. In other words, team A identified almost 2.5 times as many responsive documents as the original coders, team B identified almost three times as many, and team B identified 19 percent more than team A.

Overall, decisions for both responsiveness and nonresponsiveness made by the original team agreed with those of teams A and B 75.6 percent and 72.0 percent of the time; between teams A and B, the agreement was 70.3 percent.[43] However, because this percentage of overall agreement (one of many ways to measure what might be thought of as "overlap") is primarily based on the much larger number of documents judged to be nonresponsive, it arguably obscures how inconsistent the teams were on identifying just the specific documents that needed to be produced.

Perhaps a more helpful way to look at this issue is by how often the teams were in agreement on responsive documents only—in other words, the percentage of "specific agreement on positives."[44] Of the documents judged as responsive either by the original reviewers or by team A, both teams were in agreement on positives 28.0 percent of the time (the ideal is 100 percent). The corresponding rate for the original reviewers and team B was 27.3 percent; for team A and team B, it was 43.8 percent.

A related way of looking at overlap is through the use of Jaccard's index of similarity, defined as the number of responsive documents identified by *both* teams divided by the total number of responsive documents identified by *any* team. The values for the indexes between the original reviewers and team A, the original reviewers and team B, and teams A and B were 16.3 percent, 15.8 percent, and 28.1 percent, respectively. Such results should be viewed in light of the fact that a Jaccard's index of less than 50 percent implies that two sets of reviewers disagreed more than half the time with each other's assessment of what was relevant. Though it is not possible to determine which team (original, A, or B) made better decisions, it is quite

[42] Roitblat, Kershaw, and Oot, 2010.

[43] These percentages are calculated by summing the number of documents both teams agreed were responsive and the number of documents both teams agreed were nonresponsive, and then dividing the sum by the total number of documents. Viewed from the opposite perspective, the frequency of disagreement ranged from one in four documents to one in almost three, depending on the coding pair being examined.

[44] The formula for calculating specific agreement on positives (here, relevant documents), also referred to as the *proportion of specific agreement*, is twice the number of instances in which both teams agreed that a document was relevant, divided by the sum of (1) twice the number of agreed relevant documents, (2) the number of documents judged as relevant by team A but not team B, and (3) the number of documents judged as relevant by team B but not team A. See, e.g., Fleiss, Levin, and Cho Paik, 2003, p. 600.

clear that there can be marked variation in review-related decisionmaking even when performed by experienced attorneys.[45]

The results of another study also suggest great variability in review decisions.[46] This work came out of the Discovery of Electronically Stored Information (DESI) workshop that focused on large-scale e-discovery at the 2011 International Conference on Artificial Intelligence and Law (ICAIL). The study examined approximately 28,000 documents using seven teams of attorneys, each team representing a different legal review service provider or law firm. All attorneys tasked with judging whether the documents were responsive to the facts of the case were trained in a similar manner and provided with the same set of instructions. The documents were grouped into slightly more than 12,000 "families," similar to what might be the result of email threading or clustering techniques discussed previously. A family of two documents might, for example, consist of an email and its one attachment (36 percent of the families had only a single document, 52 percent had two or three, and approximately 1 percent had seven or more). As would be true in many actual document reviews, the rule was that, if any of the documents in a family were judged to be responsive, the entire family was coded as responsive. In the end, the seven teams differed significantly on the percentage of families determined to be responsive, ranging from a low of 23.1 percent to a high of 54.2 percent.[47] The overall agreement between various pairs of reviewing teams ranged from 65.5 percent to 84.9 percent.[48]

Somewhat better results were reported in an earlier study that used five different groups of reviewers to examine the same 10,000 emails for responsiveness.[49] The groups' assessments of the number of responsive documents within the set ranged from 39.6 percent to 57.7 percent. In other words, one group of reviewers believed they found 46 percent more responsive documents than did another group with similar training and background.

Another telling study emerged from a venue commonly used for presenting empirical research related to discovery issues: the Legal Track of the Text REtrieval Conference (TREC), an initiative led by the National Institute of Standards and Technology (NIST, part of the U.S. Department of Commerce).[50] The study used second- and third-year law students to conduct reviews for relevance, after being instructed in a process that replicated what they might encounter in an actual discovery review. A prior research project had used much the same data, type of reviewers, and instructions for a similar relevancy review, so the output of that earlier work, coupled with that from this study, could provide a useful means of comparing the decisions made by different sets of reviewers.

---

[45] There is some evidence that attorneys produce *worse* results than nonattorneys in review for relevancy decisions. See Voorhees, 2000, which assessed the performance of information analysts rather than attorneys, all receiving the same training and working under identical conditions. See Wang and Soergel, 2010, pp. 1–2; and Efthimiadis and Hotchkiss, 2008, p. 2, which shows that relevancy determinations are equally accurate (or inaccurate) whether the reviewer has a law background or not.

[46] Barnett and Godjevac, 2011.

[47] For two of the teams, 20–30 percent of the documents were judged to be relevant, the percentages ranged between 30 and 40 percent for three teams, and two teams found 50 percent or more of the documents to be relevant.

[48] Defined as the number of documents both teams agreed were responsive plus the number of documents both teams agreed were nonresponsive, then the sum divided by the total number of documents in the set.

[49] Barnett et al., 2009.

[50] Oard, Hedin, et al., 2009.

About ten documents judged to be relevant and about ten judged to be nonrelevant in the prior study were selected in each of 12 different topic categories and shown to the later set of reviewers. Of 116 documents previously coded as relevant in the earlier project, just 62.1 percent were now identified as relevant to some degree (including ones felt to be in a "grey area").[51] Of 120 previously coded nonrelevant documents, 18.3 percent had now been identified as relevant.

A separate study that employed a somewhat similar approach had assessors judge the relevance of about 50 documents in 40 different categories, of which about half had been found to be relevant by other assessors.[52] The agreement on positives was less than 30 percent for 12 of the 40 topics and less than 70 percent for 31 of the topics. Although one might argue that the use of law students rather than experienced attorneys in the two studies described above to conduct the review tests might play a role in the reduced rate of agreement, it should be kept in mind that many of the contract attorneys used for high-volume review are, in fact, relatively recent law school graduates.

Taken together, this body of research shows that groups of human reviewers exhibit significant inconsistency when examining the same set of documents for responsiveness under conditions similar to those in large-scale reviews. Is the high level of disagreement among reviewers with similar backgrounds and training reported in all of these studies simply a function of the fact that determinations of responsiveness or relevance are so subjective that reasonable and informed people can be expected to disagree on a routine basis? Evidence suggests that this is not the case.[53] Human error in applying the criteria for inclusion, not a lack of clarity in the document's meaning or ambiguity in how the scope of the production demand should be interpreted, appears to be the primary culprit. In other words, people make mistakes, and, according to the evidence, they make them regularly when it comes to judging relevance and responsiveness.

---

[51] An updated description of this study reported essentially similar results. See Hedin et al., 2010, pp. 33–35.

[52] Lewis, 2007.

[53] Grossman and Cormack, 2011b.

CHAPTER FIVE

Moving Beyond Eyes-On Review: The Promise of Computer-Categorized Review

We have shown that it will be difficult to achieve substantial cost savings in review solely by future reductions in the cost of labor or future increases in the rates of review. Litigant expenditures for review are unlikely to decline to levels approaching those incurred for processing if review continues to be based on visual inspection of individual documents. If e-discovery production costs are ever to be addressed in any meaningful way, then the legal community must move beyond its current reliance on eyes-on review.

Our assessment of the published research in this area suggests that computer-categorized document review has the potential to significantly reduce costs without compromising the quality of assessment when compared with large-scale reviews conducted in the traditional way. In this chapter, we draw on the research about one type of computer-categorized review—predictive coding—to describe how it works, how accurate it is, and the degree to which it might reduce the cost of review.

How Predictive Coding Works

Predictive coding, sometimes referred to as *suggestive coding*, is a process by which the computer does the heavy lifting in deciding whether documents are relevant, responsive, or privileged. This process is not to be confused with keyword-based Boolean searches or the similarity-detection technologies described in Chapter Four. Near-duplication techniques, clustering, and email threading can help provide organizational structure to the corpus of documents requiring review but do not reduce the document set that has to be reviewed by attorneys for specific aspects, such as responsiveness or privilege. Predictive coding, on the other hand, takes the very substantial next step of automatically assigning a rating (or *proximity score*) to each document to reflect how close it is to the concepts and terms found in examples of documents attorneys have already determined to be relevant, responsive, or privileged. This assignment becomes increasingly accurate as the software continues to learn from human reviewers about what is, and what is not, of interest. This score and the self-learning function are the two key characteristics that set predictive coding apart from less robust analytical techniques.[1] It should be noted at the outset that we use the term *predictive coding* throughout this monograph in a

[1] Confusion in terminology may arise because many of the methodologies underlying clustering and near-duplicate detection are also employed in some predictive-coding approaches. Some vendors may also use the term in an imprecise manner when describing the suite of services they offer for streamlining review.

generic sense as a type of computer-categorized review tool, rather than to refer to any particular methodology or commercial application.[2]

Predictive coding software can be trained for the purposes of a document review in several ways. One approach has attorneys select documents from the review set as "seeds" (or exemplars) that they have judged to be clearly fitting, or not fitting, the desired characteristics of various document categories. One category might be represented by a small group of documents highly relevant to the facts of the case and responsive to the discovery request, and another category by a small group of documents in which there is no obvious connection at all. Another approach has the application initially draw random samples from the review set for the attorneys to examine and make a decision on each selected document. Still another involves keyword or concept searches of the review set to identify small numbers of potentially relevant (or not relevant) documents for the attorneys to examine. No matter how these initial exemplars are chosen, the attorney-reviewed documents are then analyzed by the predictive-coding software, which creates a type of template to be used to screen other documents, assigns scores to each document in the review set to reflect the probability that they fit the desired template, and then draws samples of its decisions for human reviewers.[3] Attorneys then review the samples and apply their own judgment as to whether the selected documents are relevant, responsive, or privileged. Those decisions are then used by the software to refine its templates, reassess the review set, and then draw new samples. This process continues until the results are stabilized or optimized, at which point disagreement between the software's decisions and those of human reviewers should be kept to a minimum.[4]

With the application's final decisions in hand, those overseeing the review must then decide how to proceed. In the context of a review for relevance and responsiveness, for example, one option might be to assume that all documents with probability scores above a particular percentage threshold can be safely classified as relevant and responsive, all those with scores below a different percentage threshold can be safely classified as not relevant or not responsive, and only those in the middle would require eyes-on review. Another option would be to perform eyes-on review of only those documents exceeding a specific probability score in order to confirm the application's decisions, while dropping the remainder from all further work. A perhaps unlikely option would be to dispense with human review entirely, selecting a score above which all documents are sent directly to opposing counsel while those below are dropped. Ultimately, it is up to those supervising the review to decide what the appropriate cutoff points might be and where to focus the efforts of human reviewers. Any of these approaches would likely produce significant cost savings for responding litigants.

There are other review-related uses for predictive coding. One would be to use predictive coding primarily as a quality-enhancement process, in which the small number of documents

---

[2] In 2011, an e-discovery vendor received a patent for its specific approach to predictive coding, and it appears that the company claims common-law trademark rights to the term (Koblentz, 2011). However, the term appears to be widely used in the e-discovery industry to describe a variety of computer-categorized review techniques. See, e.g., Kershaw and Howie, 2010b, p. 5.

[3] For a very useful description of the analytical concepts that underlie such techniques as predictive coding, see Akers, Mason, and Mansmann, 2011.

[4] As is true with any large-scale linear review, every predictive-coding effort must draw samples from the final decision sets for the attorneys managing the review to audit the results and provide documentation of the process in the event of a challenge.

with the highest scores are sent to the attorneys most closely connected to the litigation, providing potential trial counsel with the greatest chance of finding a potentially hot document during the review, while those with lower scores might be sent to lower-cost contract attorneys or offshore LPOs. Another way to enhance efficiency would be conduct eyes-on review on only the documents with the highest scores, initially providing those to opposing counsel as part of a rolling production schedule, and negotiating any need to review the remainder. Still another would be to conduct the review in a traditional manner but display the scores to the reviewer as the documents are viewed, thus supplying what amounts to an instant second opinion for the reviewer's decision. But, unless predictive coding is used to categorize a considerable fraction of the corpus of documents intended for review to cut back on the need for eyes-on examination, it will not result in significant cost savings.

As should be clear from this description, predictive coding does not take humans out of the review loop. It requires intensive attorney support throughout the process in order to advance machine learning. Ironically, for a technique that could substantially reduce discovery expenses, the best results will be achieved if the attorneys most closely involved in the case select the seed documents and review sampled extracts, effectively precluding the use of lower-cost contract attorneys or LPO vendors for these particular tasks. Moreover, attorney judgment continues to loom large in the process after the application has completed its work, with eyes-on review required, for example, to check documents of unknown relevance and responsiveness or look for privileged communications.

How Accurate Is Predictive Coding?

Though the body of research comparing the accuracy of predictive coding with that of traditional eyes-on review continues to evolve, we summarize four studies in some detail here to address the main concern about adopting a new approach to review of electronic documents—that is, that it will compromise the quality of traditional eyes-on review.[5] All of these studies offer evidence that predictive coding is at least as accurate and efficient as traditional review when the matter involves large volumes of documents.[6]

One study, already discussed in Chapter Four regarding evidence of the accuracy of human review, employed five different teams of human reviewers and a predictive-coding application to review the same set of 10,000 documents.[7] The goal was to identify how well the predictive coding replicated each team's decisions in terms of *recall* and *precision*. In information-retrieval science, *recall* is a measurement of completeness, essentially describing how well a process identifies items of specific interest, compared with the total number of such items that exist in a set of data or documents. *Precision* is a measurement of efficiency, describing

---

[5] For additional studies that examine the accuracy of various computer-categorized document-review applications, see Oard, Hedin, et al., 2009; and Hedin et al., 2010.

[6] One widely cited article (Kershaw, 2005) described a test in which the decisions of six reviewers on a set of about 20,000 documents were compared with those made by an unidentified software application. After examining documents in which the software and humans disagreed and adjusting as necessary, it was reported that the software "on average, identified more than 95 percent of the relevant documents," while the human reviewers "averaged 51.1 percent of the relevant documents." We do not include this study in our main description of predictive-coding accuracy because the article is unclear about what type of application was being tested and does not provide sufficiently detailed information about the results.

[7] Barnett et al., 2009.

how well a process identifies *only* those items of specific interest, by comparing the number of target items identified and the total number of documents retrieved. To describe the relationship between recall and precision, a statistic known as the *F-measure* calculates the harmonic mean of precision and recall. Larger F-measures indicate better overall results as measured by the balance between recall and precision. For additional explanation of recall, precision, and F-measures, as well as how such statistics are calculated, see Appendix B.

Using their team 5's original decisions regarding the responsiveness of a document as the "gold standard," the study's authors examined how well the other four teams and the application could match those decisions. A recall rate of 100 percent would mean that the set of documents the secondary reviewer (either one of the other four teams or the application) identified as responsive included *every* document that team 5 had previously identified as responsive. A precision rate of 100 percent would mean that none of the documents the secondary reviewer had identified as responsive was one that team 5 had previously identified as *not* responsive. Each of the five human review teams had looked at the same set of documents and made responsiveness decisions based on the same criteria; in theory, there should be relatively high agreement between team 1 and team 5, team 2 and team 5, and so on. The application was trained using randomly selected samples of 1,000 documents from team 5 (500 that had been previously judged as responsive and 500 that had been previously judged as nonresponsive). The application's categorization templates would thus be based on team 5's reasoning.

As shown in Table 5.1, recall rates for the first four teams versus team 5 ranged from 66 to 81 percent. Using team 3 as an example, the set of documents team 3 flagged as responsive included 80 percent of all documents team 5 had originally flagged. Precision rates for the four teams ranged from 68 to 81 percent. Again using team 3 as the example, 75 percent of the set team 3 flagged were, in fact, documents that had previously been identified as responsive by team 5. F-measures for the four teams ranged from 0.72 to 0.79.

How did the predictive coding–based review compare? As indicated previously, predictive coding does not directly make a yes-no decision about whether a document is a good match; instead, it calculates a score that represents the probability that a match has been found. It is up to those managing the process to decide what score should be used as the minimum threshold for determining whether the application had identified a responsive document. As Table 5.1 indicates, increasing the threshold level from 50 percent to 75 percent to 95 percent

Table 5.1
Test of a Predictive-Coding Application and Four Review Teams

Review Comparison	F-Measure	Recall (%)	Precision (%)
Team 1 versus team 5	0.717347	66	78
Team 2 versus team 5	0.739778	81	68
Team 3 versus team 5	0.775841	80	75
Team 4 versus team 5	0.789282	77	81
Application versus team 5, 0.50 probability threshold	0.806228	99	68
Application versus team 5, 0.75 probability threshold	0.848421	93	78
Application versus team 5, 0.95 probability threshold	0.785912	71	88

SOURCE: Barnett et al., 2009, Table 6 and Table 4.

(in other words, requiring an increasingly higher probability of a match) decreases the likelihood that most of the responsive documents will have been identified (as indicated by lower recall rates) while increasing the likelihood that the group of documents flagged by the application contain few nonresponsive documents (as indicated by higher precision rates).[8] But no matter which threshold was used, the application generally performed as well as or better than each of the four human teams did based on the F-measure.

A second study was based on an actual production of 1.8 million documents, all of which had been reviewed by attorneys in the earlier case.[9] Two different teams (A and B) of experienced reviewers supplied by two legal review services vendors re-reviewed a sample of 5,000 of those documents. The decisions from the two teams were then compared with those of the attorneys in the original review and with each other. In addition, two commercial applications (designated as system C and system D), provided by different vendors and described by the study's authors as "computer-assisted categorization processes," were used to review the full set of 1.8 million documents, again for the purpose of comparing its decisions with those of the original reviewers.

Table 5.2 shows the results of both the human re-reviewers and the two software applications in comparison to the decisions of the original reviewers. The comparison is instructive: The computerized process achieved better results by almost every measure. Overall agreement (as indicated by the Jaccard's index) and agreement on positives were higher for both system C and system D than those reported for either team A or team B. Recall rates were roughly similar (team B had a slight edge over system D, and team A had a slight edge over system C), but precision rates were much better for the two computerized systems, which resulted in higher F-measures for the automated processes. Although predictive coding is not perfect, it is clearly no worse than what currently passes for a reasonable approach to review large-scale productions, at least based on the existing research.

Two issues must be kept in mind when interpreting these results. First, the human-reviewer analysis was performed on a set of 5,000 sampled documents, while the predictive-coding process was conducted on the far larger review set. Second, although the study used the original reviewers' decisions as the gold standard for comparison, there is no guarantee that those decisions were correct ones.

In a third study, a vendor reported that its application had been tested on 47,650 documents that had already been subjected to eyes-on review, with 4,624 of the documents originally judged as responsive.[10] The decisions of the predictive-coding system returned 5,579 potentially responsive documents. Both the software and original attorney review team had identified 3,048 documents as responsive and 40,495 as nonresponsive, for an overall agreement rate of 91.4 percent (see Table 5.3). Agreement on positives (see the formula in "Accuracy of

---

[8] In this particular study, responsive documents in the review set had already been identified by team 5, which provided a straightforward means of calculating rates of recall and precision using different threshold levels for the application. In an actual review using predictive coding, such rates would have to be estimated through sampling of the review set. The information yielded by such sampling would provide a basis for deciding on the most appropriate threshold setting. One commonly employed way to visualize how these measures would vary depending on the setting is through the use of a *receiver operating characteristic* (ROC) curve, in which recall and precision are plotted against various threshold values. For additional information regarding how ROC plots are used to conduct cost-benefit analyses for search and retrieval tools, see Roitblat, 2006, pp. 4–6.

[9] Roitblat, Kershaw, and Oot, 2010.

[10] Equivio, 2009a.

Table 5.2
Relative Accuracy of Human Re-Reviewers (Teams A and B) and Computer-Categorized Review Applications (Systems C and D) Compared with That of Original Reviewers

Review Comparison	Team A Versus Original Reviewers (Sample Only)	Team B Versus Original Reviewers (Sample Only)	System C Versus Original Reviewers	System D Versus Original Reviewers
Both agreed on responsiveness	238	263	78,617	90,416
Only original reviewers judged as responsive	250	225	92,908	81,109
Only team or system judged as responsive	971	1,175	211,403	216,359
Both agreed on nonresponsiveness	3,541	3,337	1,430,684	1,425,728
Total in review set	5,000	5,000	1,813,612	1,813,612
Overall agreement (%)	75.6	72.0	83.2	83.6
Jaccard's index (%)	16.3	15.8	20.5	23.3
Agreement on positives (%)	28.0	27.3	34.1	37.8
Recall (%)	48.8	53.9	45.8	52.7
Precision (%)	19.7	18.3	27.1	29.5
F-measure	0.280	0.273	0.340	0.378

SOURCE: Roitblat, Kershaw, and Oot, 2010.

Table 5.3
Example of Predictive-Coding Decisionmaking Compared with That of Human Reviewers

Subject Matter	Reviewer Judged as Responsive	Reviewer Judged as Not Responsive	Total
Software judged as responsive	3,048	2,531	5,579
Software judged as not responsive	1,576	40,495	42,071
Total	4,624	43,026	47,650

SOURCE: Equivio, 2009a, Table 1.

Traditional Review" in Chapter Four) was 59.7 percent. Both scores were higher than those in three reported studies comparing decisions made by human review teams described in Chapter Four.[11]

A test was then performed on the 4,107 documents for which the two approaches differed in their decisions. A sample of 190 documents was drawn from that set for a human referee to judge relevance independently, without knowledge of any prior decisions. The referee agreed with the software's determination of relevance for these mixed-result documents 77.4 percent

[11] Roitblat, Kershaw, and Oot, 2010; Barnett and Godjevac, 2011; Lewis, 2007.

of the time, suggesting that the predictive-coding approach performed a higher quality of review than what took place in the original coding effort.

Finally, a fourth study used the massive Enron document set discussed in Chapter Four.[12] Five different "reviews" were conducted on the more than 800,000 emails and their separate attachments, each with a different definition of relevance (referred to as a "topic" in the study). One topic, for example, involved a request for

> [a]ll documents or communications that describe, discuss, refer to, report on, or relate to any intentions, plans, efforts, or activities involving the alteration, destruction, retention, lack of retention, deletion, or shredding of documents or other evidence, whether in hard-copy or electronic form. (p. 6, Table 4)

Each topic was tested using two different computer-categorized review applications. The relevancy decisions of these automated review techniques were then sampled and the results subsequently examined by human assessors, who, depending on the topic, might have been drawn from staff at professional review services or were volunteers (primarily law students, with some attorneys and legal professionals). When an application's judgment of relevance conflicted with that of the assessors, there was an opportunity to appeal the disagreement to a *topic authority*, a person playing the role of a senior attorney who would have been overseeing the review and exercising professional legal responsibility had the test been an actual production. Thus, each test would involve a comparison between an application's decisions and the adjusted assessor decisions (i.e., all unappealed assessor decisions plus the topic authority's rulings for those that were appealed).

Because they had been subjected to an appeal process, the set of adjusted assessor decisions were used as a gold standard for gauging not only the technological application's performance (see results described in the preceding paragraph) but also how well the human assessors performed originally. As can be seen in Table 5.4, recall was better for the applications in three of the five topics, precision better in all five, and the F-measure better in four of the five. In most instances, when the human review performance exceeded that of the application, the difference was a slight one.

Because human reviewers were the original source for what was ultimately used as the gold standard for comparisons, it may seem counterintuitive that the recall and precision rates presented in Table 5.4 for those reviewers not only do not approach 100 percent but are often in the 20- to 30-percent range. The explanation is that the topic authority sided with the application's decision in 89 percent of the appeals.[13] A subsequent review of the topic authority's appellate decisions by a person acting as a type of supreme court agreed with the topic authority's call nearly 90 percent of the time.[14]

As all these studies demonstrate, predictive coding has the capability of identifying at least as many documents of interest as an eyes-on examination in a large-scale review, though it is certainly not perfect in this regard and performance appears to vary depending on the application's methodology and the types of documents being examined. In addition, it has been argued that the studies comparing human reviewers with predictive-coding applications

[12] Grossman and Cormack, 2011b. See also Klimt and Yang, 2004.

[13] Grossman and Cormack, 2011b, p. 3 and Table 1.

[14] Grossman and Cormack, 2011b, pp. 3–5 and Table 2.

Table 5.4
Comparison of Human Reviewers and Computer-Categorized Review Applications, Adjudicated Decisions Used as Gold Standard

Topic	Review Comparison	Recall (%)	Precision (%)	F-Measure
1	Application A	77.8	91.2	0.840
	Humans (mostly law students)	75.6	5.0	0.095
2	Application A	67.3	88.4	0.764
	Humans (mostly law students)	79.9	26.7	0.400
3	Application A	86.5	69.2	0.769
	Humans (mostly professionals)	25.2	12.5	0.167
4	Application B	76.2	84.4	0.801
	Humans (mostly professionals)	36.9	25.5	0.302
5	Application A	76.1	90.7	0.828
	Humans (mostly professionals)	79.0	89.0	0.837

SOURCE: Grossman and Cormack, 2011a, Table 7.

and concluding that an automated approach works just as well, "though suggestive, are not conclusive," in part because the types of reviewers used during these experiments are said to be of "highly variable reliability."[15] But, although no experimental setting to assess the relative qualities of human or computer-categorized review can be completely free of "unrealism and artificiality,"[16] the empirical evidence that is currently available does suggest that similar results in large-scale reviews would be achieved with either approach.

How Cost-Effective Is Predictive Coding?

The costs of predictive coding–based review include several elements: the costs associated with the use of relatively experienced counsel for machine-learning tasks and quality-control samples, a vendor's charges for its predictive-coding services or licensing of its software, and the costs of traditional eyes-on review conducted on residual documents determined to be suitable for contract attorneys and the like. How do these costs compare with those of linear review?

Unfortunately, the answer is not entirely clear at the moment. Predictive coding is a nascent technology in the context of legal discovery, and there simply are not many data points to use when comparing this process with the way litigants currently conduct reviews of electronic documents. It is almost certainly true that predictive coding will save money over the classic model of well-paid associates carefully reading each page in document after document in large-scale production. But it is difficult to estimate the magnitude of those savings. Any

[15] Webber, 2011, p. 1, critiquing Roitblat, Kershaw, and Oot, 2010, and Grossman and Cormack, 2011b. Webber argues that, to be able to draw "firmer conclusions on the relative merits of the manual and automated review," the same topic authority should be used for evaluating the decisions of both approaches and that the review, even in an experimental setting, "be conducted according to industry standards" similar to those found in actual discovery productions.

[16] Webber, 2011, p. 6.

assessment of relative costs must compare predictive coding with *enhanced* eyes-on review—that is, human review in a contemporary document production that is assisted by near-duplicate detection, better management of workflow with quality-control procedures, email threading, pre-review sampling, the use of experienced vendors specializing in large-scale review, clustering analysis, an increased reliance on contract attorneys and LPOs, and bulk-coding decisions. Moreover, it is also important to factor into the comparison all the various cost components of both human and computer-categorized approaches, such as licensing fees, vendor charges, the total costs of attorney services (both for developing the training set of documents and for conducting review on the residual set), and quality-assurance measures.

There are few published reports of predictive coding in actual discovery productions that provide sufficiently detailed cost comparisons with human-review approaches.[17] One reason for the dearth of empirical data in this regard may be the traditional reluctance of organizations and attorneys to publicly reveal the details of their litigation expenditures. Another may be methodological difficulties involved in benchmarking the costs of computer-categorized document-review strategies against those of human approaches. And it may not be possible to talk about "typical" cost savings because the relative efficiencies are not uniform but instead vary by case. One attempt to gather at least some benchmarks in this area was the eDiscovery Institute Survey on Predictive Coding that surveyed organizations known to be active in the e-discovery marketplace.[18] Nine respondents who identified themselves as offering predictive-coding services answered the following question:

> As compared to a linear review of the same content after duplicate consolidation, after culling based on domain name analysis of emails (e.g. excluding emails from CNNSports.com) and after email threading, what percentage of time do you estimate is saved by predictive coding when used to select responsive records?

Four of the respondents reported average savings of 40 percent, while three provided estimates ranging from 50 to 65 percent (the other two estimates were 3 percent and 80 percent). It is difficult to interpret these results, in part because the question was posed in terms of time savings, which could refer to attorney hours or project duration. If reviewer time is what was assumed by respondents, the question may not fully address the issue of whether predictive coding saves money, especially if vendor charges or licensing fees are substantial enough to offset any reduction in the number of hours of eyes-on document examination.[19] Moreover, it

---

[17] For examples of informal reports of cost savings, see Lacey, Tanner, and Moeskops, undated (a review employing predictive coding resulted in total costs that were just a "fraction" of what a human-based approach would require); and Driver, 2011 (interviewing David J. Laing, describing a review in which part of the document set was analyzed using predictive coding while the remainder involved human reviewers; reported costs of production using computer-categorization appear to be about 20 percent of those for the traditional approach).

[18] Kershaw and Howie, 2010b.

[19] Given that predictive coding is still an evolving technology offered by relatively few vendors, the size of that offset is still an open question:

> How predictive coding services will be priced in the future remains uncertain. As demonstrated by fees for de-duplication services, vendors tend to charge by the cost savings to the firm—not the effort it takes the vendor to provide the service. This means that even if use of predictive coding would cost significantly less than manual review, vendor fees eventually could reduce the amount of savings. (Whittingham, Rippey, and Perryman, 2011, p. 14)

is unclear whether these savings estimates were based on careful comparative analyses of actual reviews or simply impressions of what might be possible under ideal conditions.

Nevertheless, the responses do provide insight into the potential of predictive coding, both what it can do and what it cannot. Six of the nine respondents reported observed *minimum* savings (however defined) of between 20 percent and 30 percent (the other three reported savings of 0 percent, 10 percent, and 50 percent), again suggesting that predictive coding may not be the solution for every type of review set.[20] Indeed, one respondent noted that the effectiveness of predictive coding is not always constant and depends on the software being "successfully trained and used" and that, "[o]ccasionally, due to poorly-defined issues, inconsistent tagging by the expert, or exceptionally low richness (less than 1%), the statistical model detects and notifies the user that training is ineffective. . . ."[21] In terms of *maximum* observed results, seven of the nine respondents reported savings of 77 percent or more, which would, assuming that vendor charges and other associated expenditures do not markedly offset those savings, meet the goal set forth at the outset of Chapter Four for reducing review costs.

Another study of interest does not directly analyze cost differences between human review and predictive coding, but it provides information about the time consumed in the two processes to allow informal estimates of the magnitude of savings. We have already reported on aspects of that study, which assessed the relative accuracy of human versus predictive-coding systems.[22] The vendor tested its application against 47,650 documents that had already been subjected to review. The original review reportedly required seven weeks of effort to go through the documents one by one. As part of the software's training for the subsequent test, 25 samples of 50 documents each were drawn from the review set periodically for relevance determination, in total requiring 18 hours of attorney review for all 1,250 items (a rate of about 70 documents per hour per reviewer). Once the training samples were incorporated into the software's decisionmaking process, 5,579 potentially responsive documents were identified. The specific cost savings were not reported, but a rough measure of magnitude can be gleaned from the information that was supplied in the publication. If the original review had been performed at a rate similar to one for the training review, the 47,650 documents would have required 686 hours of attorney time. If only the approximately 5,600 documents identified as relevant by the application were sent to reviewers (and those that were not were dropped), and if the review team continued to perform at 70 documents per hour, then 80 hours of residual review would have been needed. Thus, the application of predictive coding would have saved an estimated 86 percent in attorney review hours (98 hours for both training and residual review versus 686 hours originally). Although these estimates do not include the costs of the vendor's services, and the potential reduction in hours would be strongly influenced by the threshold probability scores used for determining potential matches, the total savings are nevertheless likely to be considerable.

---

[20] One possible reason for such a wide range of answers is that what is likely to be the most expensive component of computer-categorized document review—the volume of documents requiring eyes-on examination before, during, and after machine processing—will vary depending on the nature of the data, the questions that are being asked, the estimated proportion of desired documents within the review set, the specific methodology used for predictive coding, the workflow approach chosen to utilize the predictive-coding results, and the level of confidence in the results that those overseeing the review are willing to tolerate.

[21] Kershaw and Howie, 2010b, p. 14.

[22] Equivio, 2009a.

It is possible that such calculations are on the conservative side because the rate of review for residual sets may be higher than the average rate of a linear review of unorganized documents. One study, for example, described an extremely expeditious eyes-on review following a computer-categorized review application's processing of an email-rich set of documents.[23] The documents were organized by decreasing order of the application's score for relevance, so the reviewers would initially be seeing document after document that was likely to be relevant. The effective rate was claimed to be 20 documents per minute as a result. In contrast, an attorney conducing an unstructured, linear review might not come across a relevant document until dozens of nonrelevant ones had been examined, perhaps requiring a shifting of mental gears to make sense of what was being displayed on the screen.

It should be noted that our interests here are solely in cost savings that have been *clearly* documented for the use of computer-categorization techniques in large-scale *reviews*. Some vendor press releases and marketing materials have claimed that predictive coding yields significant savings in the context of such reviews, but they provide little information as to how those savings were calculated. In addition, some large organizations and law firms are using applications employing analytic strategies similar to predictive coding as tools for analyzing large document sets and, reportedly, reducing labor costs as a result.[24] However, these uses appear to be for internal analysis of ESI (such as for developing litigation strategies or locating specific documents of interest) rather than for confirming relevance, responsiveness, or privilege as part of a discovery production.

---

[23] Cormack and Mojdeh, 2010.

[24] See, e.g., Recommind, undated; Roach, 2012.

CHAPTER SIX

Barriers to Computer-Categorized Reviews

We have shown that predictive coding in large-scale discovery review has the potential to yield significant cost savings without compromising quality as compared with that provided by a human review. If this is indeed the case, it is reasonable to ask why it is not being adopted by more litigants. None of the companies participating in our data collection, for example, employed a computer-categorized review strategy, despite having firsthand knowledge of how expensive review can be. Although some reported taking aggressive steps to reduce their production expenditures, such as setting up their own review shops in-house, farming work out to less expensive law firms or LPOs in the United States, or outsourcing the job overseas, they ended up using an eyes-on examination of each page in every document. Review by human eyes is still the exclusive approach for these organizations, with the exception of instances in which unique circumstances and time pressure have led to heavy reliance on traditional keyword searches to identify documents as responsive or privileged.[1]

The companies participating in our data collection do not appear to be atypical of large organizational litigants in regard to the use of computer-categorized document review strategies. A search for published accounts of the use of such technologies in the legal press and popular media suggests that few litigants are comfortable with the idea of openly employing predictive coding and similar approaches for the purposes of review. The search returned a considerable volume of vendor-generated marketing materials containing claims of how well predictive coding works under controlled conditions, numerous press releases touting the adoption of vendors' products by law firms and organizational litigants, and multiple articles discussing how some law firm clients have agreed in principle to use the methodology.[2] But, with the exception of recent reports about two federal cases that were still in the discovery stage as this monograph went to press, there were no published confirmations of actual cases with identifiable parties in which predictive coding was used as the primary means of performing a real document review. The absence of such reports does not mean that predictive coding has not been utilized for such purposes, only that any litigants and their attorneys who have employed computer categorization have been reluctant to publicly disclose their use of what some might consider untested technology.[3]

---

[1] In one case included in our study, the participating company employed Boolean keyword searches as the sole means of identifying potentially relevant and responsive documents in the review set (an eyes-on review for privilege took place following the searches).

[2] See, e.g., Equivio, 2009a; Recommind, 2010a, 2010b; and Soder, 2010.

[3] We have been told that computer-categorization techniques have, in fact, been employed in document reviews but that the use was not disclosed to opposing parties or the court. Such disclosure might be a recommended practice (see, e.g., Grimm, Bergstrom, and Kraeuter, 2011, p. 76), but there may be concerns that, with disclosure, opposing parties might

Why has the legal community resisted moving beyond linear review and gaining the potential benefits of predictive coding? We believe that there are several barriers to change, which we describe in this chapter. We also propose a possible avenue for helping to move the legal community across those barriers.

Sources of Resistance

Concerns About Recall and Precision

First is the concern about recall. If a predictive-coding approach fails to identify important responsive documents, ones that are later identified by the demanding party through some other means, the negative ramifications might run the gamut from motions to compel a new production to the seeking of sanctions based on allegations that the producing party deliberately chose a less-than-comprehensive approach in order to avoid producing damaging documents. A related concern is the issue of precision. A predictive-coding approach that found essentially all responsive documents but falsely identified a large volume of ones that were not responsive could also result in adverse outcomes ranging from an order to re-review to accusations that the producing party was engaging in "dump-truck discovery" to bury damaging documents in a sea of undifferentiated data. However, although unpleasant, the ramifications of recall and precision problems are primarily economic in nature, in which any additional expenditures required to address the shortcomings might not be markedly worse than the initial cost savings.

How would all of this play out against existing statutes and court rules? Regarding the issues of recall and precision, FRCP 26(g)(1) requires that those responding to a discovery request in a federal court case make certifications as to what is being produced:

> (g) Signing Disclosures and Discovery Requests, Responses, and Objections.
>
> (1) Signature Required; Effect of Signature. Every disclosure under Rule 26(a)(1) or (a)(3) and every discovery request, response, or objection must be signed by at least one attorney of record in the attorney's own name—or by the party personally, if unrepresented—and must state the signer's address, e-mail address, and telephone number. By signing, an attorney or party certifies that to the best of the person's knowledge, information, and belief formed after a reasonable inquiry:
>
> (A) with respect to a disclosure, it is complete and correct as of the time it is made; and
>
> (B) with respect to a discovery request, response, or objection, it is:
>
> (i) consistent with these rules and warranted by existing law or by a nonfrivolous argument for extending, modifying, or reversing existing law, or for establishing new law;

---

enlarge the scope of the demand due to a perception of lower costs, vigorous litigation over the reasonableness of the approach would ensue, or any competitive advantage enjoyed by early adopters would be negated.

> (ii) not interposed for any improper purpose, such as to harass, cause unnecessary delay, or needlessly increase the cost of litigation; and
>
> (iii) neither unreasonable nor unduly burdensome or expensive, considering the needs of the case, prior discovery in the case, the amount in controversy, and the importance of the issues at stake in the action.

In other words, counsel for a producing party would have to attest that, based on a "reasonable inquiry," the production was not made for "improper purpose" (such as to cause "unnecessary delay" or needlessly increase "the costs of litigation"), "unreasonable," "unduly burdensome," or unduly "expensive." Therefore, whether or not a production results in an undercount of responsive documents or an excess of unresponsive ones is ultimately a question of whether there was a *reasonable inquiry* into the process.

An important aspect of FRCP 26(g)(1)(B) is that perfection is not required.[4] Courts (at least federal courts) could still find the use of predictive-coding technologies in the review process to be appropriate even if errors, such as shortfalls in recall or shortfalls in precision, occurred. To obtain such a finding, counsel for the producing party would have to make a convincing argument that his or her inquiries into the underlying methodology and the ultimate results of the computer-categorized review were reasonable ones and that the costs required to completely eliminate any shortfalls in recall or precision would be out of proportion to any benefit of the additional information.[5]

Review for Privileged, Confidential, or Sensitive Materials

Another barrier to overcome is that attorneys may not be confident that predictive coding will identify documents containing privileged, confidential, or sensitive information. Determining whether a document being examined is both relevant and responsive to a demand for production—a task that appears to be well within the capabilities of predictive coding—is only one aspect of review. Can a predictive-coding application take the next step and make a determination of privilege or some other aspect that might preclude disclosure? Some lawyers, even those who are open to the idea of predictive coding, are not convinced that it can, although this fear appears to be a reflection of risk aversion rather than specific concerns about the technology.[6]

---

[4] See, e.g., *Pension Comm. of the Univ. of Montreal Pension Plan v. Banc of Am. Sec., LLC*, 685 F.Supp.2d 456 (S.D.N.Y. 2010, at 461) ("In an era where vast amounts of electronic information is available for review, discovery in certain cases has become increasingly complex and expensive. Courts cannot and do not expect that any party can meet a standard of perfection").

[5] FRCP 26(b)(2)(C) states the following:

> (C) When Required. On motion or on its own, the court must limit the frequency or extent of discovery otherwise allowed by these rules or by local rule if it determines that: . . .
>
> (iii) the burden or expense of the proposed discovery outweighs its likely benefit, considering the needs of the case, the amount in controversy, the parties' resources, the importance of the issues at stake in the action, and the importance of the discovery in resolving the issues.

[6] The idea of employing technology to assist in making privilege determinations is by no means a recent development. Keyword searches and other computerized methodologies have been used for quite some time to flag electronic information as potentially containing attorney-client communications, looking for such indications as specific email senders and recipients, variants of current and former attorneys' names, email domains associated with legal services (such as xyzlawfirm.com), and key words (e.g., "attorney," "counsel," or "privileged") (see Kubacki, Lange, and Meadows, 2011).

These concerns are not likely to be ones of *overinclusion*; documents identified as privileged by predicting coding, for example, could be confirmed with eyes-on review and any automatically generated privilege log amended as needed without markedly increasing the overall costs of review (the set of documents claimed to be privileged in a production is usually far smaller than the overall volume of documents found to be both relevant and responsive). Instead, the qualms are about the *false negatives*, the documents that were *not* identified by the predictive-coding application as privileged (but should have been) and were subsequently produced. A waiver triggered by releasing such privileged information could have disastrous consequences, including losing the case, adverse impacts on other litigation, and charges of malpractice. Disclosing confidential or sensitive information, such as valuable trade secrets, because of a failure to seek protective orders could have equally negative ramifications.

Existing statutes and court rules protect parties from waiver if the disclosure was inadvertent and if reasonable steps were taken to prevent the release. FRE 502(b) describes the conditions under which a disclosure of privileged or protected materials would not be considered a waiver:

> (b) Inadvertent disclosure—When made in a Federal proceeding or to a Federal office or agency, the disclosure does not operate as a waiver in a Federal or State proceeding if:
>
> (1) the disclosure is inadvertent;
>
> (2) the holder of the privilege or protection took reasonable steps to prevent disclosure; and
>
> (3) the holder promptly took reasonable steps to rectify the error, including (if applicable) following Federal Rule of Civil Procedure 26(b)(5)(B).

As such, a party would be protected from waiver if the disclosure were *inadvertent* and if *reasonable steps* had been taken to prevent the release. The Advisory Committee Notes to FRE 502(b) explained that assessing whether a disclosure constituted a waiver would be based on "a set of non-determinative guidelines that vary from case to case," but one mentioned was the "reasonableness of the precautions taken." Could such precautions include reliance on technologies similar to predictive coding? Certainly, the advisory committee thought that it would be possible to defend such a practice:

> Depending on the circumstances, a party that uses advanced analytical software applications and linguistic tools in screening for privilege and work product may be found to have taken "reasonable steps" to prevent inadvertent disclosure.[7]

This language clearly invites litigants to at least consider the idea of employing "advanced analytical software applications and linguistic tools," such as predictive coding, when conducting privilege review. Whether or not a judge facing such questions in an actual case would be influenced by the nonbinding advisory notes remains to be seen. However, it is clear that, as

[7] FRE 502(b) advisory comm. nn., revised November 28, 2007.

was true for FRCP 26, FRE 502(b) does not require an error-free process, only a reasonable one.[8]

As for predictive coding's ability to identify confidential or sensitive information other than that involving the attorney-client privilege or protections for work product, there does not seem to be much discussion on the subject. The silence is somewhat surprising because, for some litigants, the consequences of an inadvertent disclosure of proprietary or legally protected information may be more serious than any release of attorney-client communications. Presumably, the issue is of negligible importance in computer-categorized reviews in which human attorneys are still tasked with examining documents that the software has initially identified as relevant and responsive.

Evidence from the technical literature and the legal trade press is that information-retrieval scientists and vendors see no fundamental reason that predictive coding would not be effective in detecting privilege or some other concept (in their eyes, a search for privileged or confidential documents is essentially the same as any search query). But the effectiveness of predictive coding in this instance would depend on how rich the review set is in terms of documents containing such information of interest. Teaching the system to identify documents with privileged, confidential, or sensitive passages is made far more difficult when there are few examples to use as seeds and few preliminarily identified documents to use as training samples. Future research is clearly needed to demonstrate how effective predictive coding is in identifying these types of information.

Identifying Hot Documents and Smoking Guns

Although review is conducted primarily to make sure the document set complies with the scope of the discovery request and to identify items with privileged communications or sensitive information, a secondary benefit to the producing party is that the process can help shape the litigant's own strategy. For example, reviewers may be asked to flag any document that seems particularly critical to the claims and defenses in the case so that it can be brought to the attention of lead counsel. One concern regarding computer-categorized document review is that, although the process might do a reasonably adequate job of deciding whether a document should be produced, it would be unlikely to determine whether that same document was one that might have a direct impact on the resolution of the case. As was true for privilege determinations, this should be less of a concern in instances in which human attorneys are used after the application has completed its analysis of the original document set. In addition, it is not clear whether particularly important documents are consistently flagged in current large-scale document reviews using contract attorneys or LPOs, in which the reviewers' "entire knowledge" of the case might have been based on no more than a "15 minute conversation."[9]

Review of Highly Technical or Nontext Documents

Another barrier to the use of predictive coding is the concern that the process will not work when the document set is highly technical. Many of the studies discussed in Chapter Five examined the use of the process for emails and other informal communications—a reasonable approach, given that a great deal of discoverable information is in the form of such messages—

[8] See, e.g., *Valentin v. Bank of N.Y. Mellon Corp.* 2011 WL 1466122 (S.D.N.Y. Apr. 14, 2011, at *2) ("However, the steps taken to preserve privilege need not be perfect; they must only be reasonable").

[9] Ronnie, 2011.

but there is little information about how well predictive coding works on more-complex documents, such as those found in intellectual property litigation.[10]

The types of documents subjected to review will influence the magnitude of savings realized by predictive coding. Because such coding builds heavily on semantic analysis, it would be of questionable use for documents containing images, sound, video, spreadsheets, or other nontext information. Poorly imaged versions of paper documents would share similar limitations. One option would be to subject such documents to eyes-on review even if the predictive-coding system did not identify them as potentially responsive, but doing so would have obvious cost implications if such documents made up more than a small fraction of the total review set.

Review of Relatively Small Document Sets

Predictive coding may also not be the answer for relatively modest review challenges, at least not at the present time. Some respondents to a survey of predictive-coding vendors noted that there were lower bounds beneath which predictive coding might not be useful: "not used on cases of less than 5,000 documents," "under 25,000 documents," "may be unnecessary in any case involving less than 25 GBs of ESI," "below 5,000 documents, a person can easily perform document review themselves," and "review of a document population involving just 10–20k documents could most likely be expedited more efficiently using other methods."[11] Although these thresholds differed by provider, most of the cases in our data collection appear to have been at least preliminary candidates for a predictive-coding approach: Of 38 cases in which the volume of data to be reviewed was reported, 23 exceeded 25 GB, another 11 involved reviews of 5–25 GB of information, and, of the four with less than 5 GB of reviewable data, one required examination of 190,000 documents.

Resistance of External Counsel

Another barrier to the widespread use of predictive coding could well be resistance to the idea of outside counsel motivated not so much by accuracy issues as by the potential loss of a historical revenue stream. Some interviewees reported grumblings from outside counsel when their companies decided to directly handle a fraction of the overall review process or to markedly reduce what was shipped out for review through the use of additional data processing.[12] Even without economic self-interest playing any role here, though, law firms do have ethical and professional obligations to discharge, and they may well perceive traditional review strategies as the most defensible way to prevent undesirable outcomes for their clients. In the eyes of some attorneys, at least, although a technological approach "can be a useful tool, nothing can replicate or replace a manual and comprehensive review of documents for privilege prior to production to an adversary."[13]

---

[10] Whittingham, Rippey, and Perryman, 2011, states, "It remains to be seen whether predictive coding will work well with technical documents—but it is certainly possible that predictive coding could be used here as well" (p. 13).

[11] Kershaw and Howie, 2010b, pp. 28–29.

[12] It should be noted that the use of computer-categorized review strategies would not necessarily be at odds with the interests of external law firms. One outside counsel with whom we communicated as part of this study suggested that "predictive coding is likely to help the law firms regain traction in the review space" and push "aside the review vendors" that have captured an increasing share of the market for review services.

[13] Mintz et al., 2009, p. 5.

Absence of Judicial Guidance

Perhaps the most important barrier to adopting predictive coding is the absence of widespread judicial guidance on the matter. As part of this study, we searched for cases in which the use of predictive coding or similar techniques was discussed by the court as an alternative to normal review practices. In early October 2011, we examined Westlaw's ALLCASES database of all reported state and federal judicial decisions and opinions issued since 2000 for the phrase "predictive coding," alternative names that have sometimes been used to describe the process (such as "suggestive coding" or "predictive categorization"), and terms related to certain vendors and their products that appear to employ techniques with predictive coding–like aspects. Altogether, more than 125 terms were included. Nevertheless, only a single decision delivered prior to October 2011 could be identified in which issues were discussed in relation to the use of a computerized decisionmaking process in the context of a review.[14] Though, as indicated at the outset of this chapter, judges in two cases in which discovery was still in progress as this monograph went to press have been asked to consider issues related to techniques associated with predictive coding, if litigants are looking for clear signals from the judiciary that such techniques are defensible, they will not find a wealth of authority in the case law.

The earliest of the three cases of which we are aware (and the only one that has been concluded), *Victor Stanley, Inc. v. Creative Pipe, Inc.*, clearly opened the door for employing information-retrieval methodologies that go beyond currently accepted practices, although it did not specifically mention predictive coding.[15] The issue at hand was whether possible inadequacies of keyword searches used to identify potentially privileged documents during a review

[14] Our searches returned hundreds of cases in addition to the one noted, and many involved discovery-related questions about the use of alternatives to looking at each document individually. However, we excluded those that focused on traditional keyword-type searches; discussed analytical techniques, such as concept searching, that do not categorize documents directly; discussed intellectual property rights for predictive coding; were not related to discovery; or only noted that some form of automated classification system was or could be used without considering whether the approach was reasonable. See, e.g., *In re Aspartame Antitrust Litig.*, 2011 WL 4793239 (E.D. Pa. Oct. 5, 2011; denying the award of costs for the use of "document analytics" to "separate responsive and nonresponsive documents"); *Datel Holdings Ltd. v. Microsoft Corp.*, 2011 WL 866993 (N.D. Cal. March 11, 2011; production of attorney-client–privileged documents due to a software glitch in a computer review tool was inadvertent, and steps taken to prevent disclosure were reasonable); *Mt. Hawley Ins. Co. v. Felman Prod.*, 271 F.R.D. 125 (S.D. W. Va. 2010; application failed to record results of keyword search for privileged terms; precautions taken to prevent inadvertent disclosure and lack of quality control were not reasonable); *United States v. Sensient Colors, Inc.*, 2009 WL 2905474 (D.N.J. Sep. 9, 2009; errors arising out of "commendable effort to employ a sophisticated computer program to conduct its privilege review" did not lead to waiver of privilege in light of diligent efforts and safeguards taken to prevent disclosure); *William A. Gross Const. Assocs. v. Am. Mfrs. Mut. Ins. Co.*, 256 F.R.D. 134 (S.D.N.Y. 2009; keyword searches have inherent limits requiring sampling and other quality-assurance techniques to ensure completeness); *Irwin Seating Co. v. International Business Machines Corp.*, 2008 WL 1869055 (W.D. Mich. Apr. 24, 2008; additional costs for using automated document-coding technology could not be taxed as costs against nonprevailing party); *Rhoads Indus. v. Bldg. Materials Corp. of Am.*, 254 F.R.D. 216 (E.D. Pa. 2008; keyword search for privileged documents was insufficient, and some steps taken to prevent disclosure were not reasonable, but there was no waiver of privilege); *Equity Analytics, LLC v. Lundin*, 248 F.R.D. 331 (D.D.C. 2008; a determination of whether a particular methodology, such as keyword searches, is effective would require expert testimony); *United States v. O'Keefe*, 537 F. Supp. 2d 14 (D.D.C. 2008; whether search terms will yield desired information is a complicated question involving computer technology, statistics, and linguistics and requires nonlay evidence); *Disability Rights Council of Greater Wash. v. Wash. Metro. Transit Auth.*, 242 F.R.D. 139 (D.D.C. 2007; recent scholarship argues that "concept searching" is more efficient than keyword searching and more likely to produce comprehensive results); and *Am. Library Ass'n v. United States*, 201 F. Supp. 2d 401 (E.D. Pa. 2002; not a discovery case but noted the limitations of "sophisticated automated classification systems for the statistical classification of texts" based on "artificial intelligence").

[15] 250 F.R.D. 251 (D. Md. 2008).

(and any shortcomings of measures taken for quality assurance following those searches) would waive attorney-client privilege for a set of items inadvertently produced.

The magistrate overseeing the discovery process in the case initially discussed potential alternatives to traditional keyword searches, such as "probabilistic search models," "Bayesian classifiers," "fuzzy search models," and "concept and categorization tools," noting that further advancements were expected in developing cost-effective and reliable methodologies for a variety of e-discovery tasks as a result of such projects as the Legal Track of TREC (see Chapter Four).

The magistrate went on to indicate that whatever methodology is used must be selected with "utmost care" because of the potential consequences of waving attorney-client privilege or work-product protections, with "careful advance planning" by persons qualified to design search methodologies, the implementation tested for quality assurance, and an explanation prepared for the rationale for choosing a certain approach.[16] Understanding the "literature describing the strengths and weaknesses of various methodologies" and being able to support the approach chosen based on expert evidence is critical to a judicial finding that the method was a reasonable one:

> The message to be taken from *O'Keefe*, *Equity Analytics*, and this opinion is that when parties decide to use a particular ESI search and retrieval methodology, they need to be aware of literature describing the strengths and weaknesses of various methodologies, such as The Sedona Conference Best Practices . . . and select the one that they believe is most appropriate for its intended task. Should their selection be challenged by their adversary, and the court be called upon to make a ruling, then they should expect to support their position with affidavits or other equivalent information from persons with the requisite qualifications and experience, based on sufficient facts or data and using reliable principles or methodology.[17]

Although this opinion might have opened the door, no one has publicly stepped through it, at least not until recently. Prior to 2012, there were simply no judicial decisions that squarely approved or disapproved of the use of predictive coding or similar machine-learning techniques for review purposes, despite a span of more than three years since the enactment of FRE 502 and the publication of the *Victor Stanley* decision. But, in December 2011, a discovery conference for a putative class action[18] in the Southern District of New York was held in which the parties indicated to the court that they were exploring the idea of allowing the defendant (who was responding to the plaintiff's demand for ESI production) to employ a predictive-coding approach with the goal of markedly reducing the volume of a collection of about 3 million documents prior to conducting an eyes-on review for relevance, responsiveness, privilege, and confidentiality.[19] At a conference held in January 2012, the parties continued to indicate their general agreement on the use of a predictive-coding approach, though the plaintiffs expressed concerns about the details of how the technology would be trained, employed, and tested. At a status conference in early February, these issues were discussed with the magistrate to whom

---

[16] 250 F.R.D. at 262.

[17] 250 F.R.D. at 261, fn. 10.

[18] *Da Silva Moore v. Publicis Groupe*, No. 1:11-cv-01279, S.D.N.Y., February 24, 2012.

[19] See "Opinion and Order," *Da Silva Moore v. Publicis Groupe*, No. 1:11-cv-01279, S.D.N.Y., February 24, 2012, pp. 5–6.

the case had been referred for general pretrial supervision. The magistrate then requested that the parties develop a protocol detailing various aspects of the process based on rulings he had made during the conference.[20] Subsequently, the parties jointly submitted a proposed protocol to the court, which was reduced to a stipulation and order by the magistrate. Despite the joint nature of the submission, the plaintiffs objected to the protocol order in its entirety and moved the assigned district judge to reverse the magistrate's rulings made at the February status conference.[21] The plaintiffs argued that the use of what they claimed was untested technology would effectively prevent the defendant from being able to certify that its production was complete and correct. Moreover, the plaintiffs argued that no formal evidence of predictive coding's scientific reliability had been submitted by the defendants and that, therefore, the magistrate had no foundation for the ruling that approved its use.

On February 24, the magistrate issued an opinion that discussed the plaintiffs' unresolved issues about the predictive-coding aspects of the case.[22] The magistrate noted that, although the plaintiff's objections were actually to be decided by the case's assigned district judge, "a few comments [were] in order." As to the question of certification, the magistrate suggested that, in "large-data cases like this, involving over three million emails, no lawyer using any search method could honestly certify that its production is 'complete.'" More important is the fact that the magistrate argued that there is actually no provision in the FRCP that requires certification of completeness by a party in response to a document-production demand. The magistrate also stated that there was no need to conduct a formal hearing into the reliability of predictive coding, at least not in the same way that a court might examine the reliability of expert testimony proposed for admission at trial. Finally, the magistrate advised that the plaintiff's concerns about reliability and accuracy were "premature" and more "appropriate for resolution during or after the process," when discovery would be complete and such metrics as recall or precision could be calculated.

The magistrate's opinion received wide attention in the legal media not because of its effect on the parties in the specific case before the court but instead because of the implications for the larger legal community that arise from his discussion in a section titled "Further Analysis and Lessons for the Future." The judge set forth a lengthy and detailed argument that explained the basics behind predictive coding, described how computer-categorization approaches compare in terms of recall and precision rates with traditional keyword searches and in terms of accuracy and consistency with human reviewers. He concluded that lawyers should understand that "computer-assisted review is an available tool and should be seriously considered for use in large-data-volume cases where it may save the producing party (or both parties) significant amounts of legal fees in document review." Though acknowledging that "computer-assisted review is not a magic, Staples-Easy-Button, solution appropriate for all cases," the use of predictive coding in the instant case would be

> appropriate considering: (1) the parties' agreement, (2) the vast amount of ESI to be reviewed . . . , (3) the superiority of computer-assisted review to the available alternatives (i.e., linear

---

[20] Doherty, 2012. See also "Transcript of Proceedings re: Conference Held on 2/8/2012 Before Magistrate Judge Andrew J. Peck," *Da Silva Moore v. Publicis Groupe*, No. 1:11-cv-01279, S.D.N.Y., February 8, 2012.

[21] "Plaintiffs' Rule 72(A) Objection to the Magistrate's February 8, 2012 Discovery Rulings," *Da Silva Moore v. Publicis Groupe*, No. 1:11-cv-01279, S.D.N.Y., February 22, 2012.

[22] "Opinion and Order," *Da Silva Moore v. Publicis Groupe*, No. 1:11-cv-01279, S.D.N.Y., February 24, 2012.

> manual review or keyword searches), (4) the need for cost effectiveness and proportionality under Rule 26(b)(2)(C), and (5) the transparent process proposed by [the defendant].

Though the magistrate was correct in noting that the case produced the "first Opinion dealing with predictive coding," *Da Silva Moore* cannot be considered a definitive statement from the bench that the *results* of an actual computer-categorized document review have passed judicial scrutiny or that the process constituted *reasonable steps* taken to prevent inadvertent disclosure of privileged or protected materials. Neither of those issues has been squarely addressed as of this writing. Indeed, in early March 2012, the parties jointly requested that the court stay the execution of the protocol pending the district judge's decision regarding the plaintiffs' objections—a request that, if granted, would essentially halt all activity related to predictive coding.[23] When this monograph went to press, there had been no formal ruling on the plaintiff's objections, pretrial discovery had not been completed, and, in fact, there were no indications that any of the collected documents had been subjected to a predictive-coding process as anticipated by the joint protocol.

And, in an ongoing antitrust class action filed in the Northern District of Illinois,[24] plaintiffs demanding a document production have moved for an order *requiring* the defendants to employ a technology with features similar to predictive coding as the initial means of identifying relevant and responsive documents.[25] The plaintiffs have argued that the use of a traditional Boolean approach would produce results that would be inferior to those yielded by a concept-oriented search. As of this writing, the judge in the case has not ruled on the motion.

Inertia

It is also true that many attorneys would be uncomfortable with the idea of being an early adopter when the potential downside risks appear to be so large. Few lawyers would want to be placed in the uncomfortable position of having to argue that a predictive-coding strategy reflects "reasonable precautions to prevent disclosure" in the words of FRE 502 when no one else seems to be using it. In addition, the effort needed to become familiar with the "literature describing the strengths and weaknesses of various methodologies," as well as the costs of obtaining expert testimony that would be "based on sufficient facts or data and using reliable principles or methodology," may be less than attractive to counsel already under pressure to address a client's review needs in the most straightforward and expeditious manner.

There may come a day when experts will not be needed to defend the underlying concepts behind predictive coding—the same way that affidavits from General Electric scientists are not required every time an X-ray of a broken arm is entered into evidence today. However, at the present time, such testimony would be a likely necessity. There may also be professional ethical obligations that trump FRE 502's mechanisms for reducing the risks of disclosing privileged communications; although a judge ruling on waiver might have no significant concerns about the use of a predictive-coding strategy, the client might not perceive any public release of information it considers to be highly sensitive in the same favorable light.

---

[23] "Endorsed Letter Addressed to Magistrate Judge Andrew J. Peck from Jeffrey W. Brecher," *Da Silva Moore v. Publicis Groupe*, No. 1:11-cv-01279, S.D.N.Y., March 1, 2012. The magistrate immediately denied the request.

[24] *Kleen Prods., LLC v. Packaging Corp. of Am.*, Docket 1:10-cv-05711, N.D. Ill., February 13, 2012.

[25] See "Plaintiffs' Reply Memorandum of Law for Evidentiary Hearing," *Kleen Prods., LLC v. Packaging Corp. of Am.*, Docket 1:10-cv-05711, N.D. Ill., February 13, 2012.

How to Overcome These Barriers

What would it take to break the current logjam and bring predictive coding and other computer-categorized review strategies into the mainstream? We believe that the most effective solution would be for forward-thinking, sophisticated organizational litigants to take a leap of faith and decide at the start of selected cases that their review obligations will be discharged using predictive-coding technology and to do so in a most public and transparent manner. The decisions would have to be made in light of the potential risks and additional expense of being on the cutting edge of legal technology, including the possibility that an inadvertent disclosure of some privileged or protected materials might be considered an unretractable waiver or that a court might subsequently order the review to be redone in the traditional way. The motivation for taking this step could not be any expectation of reducing review expenditures in the immediate case; instead, it would be the hope that a successful demonstration and subsequent judicial approval would lead to the routine use of the technology in large-scale reviews, accompanied by long-term cost savings for all litigants.

The effort required would not be trivial. At the outset of a case, a litigant willing to expend its time and money to help improve the civil pretrial process would need to identify competent experts who would be able to knowledgeably testify about the known limitations of human reviewers, the shortcomings of current approaches based solely on keyword searches, and the documented effectiveness of predictive coding in performing various review tasks. The litigant would also have to subject the results of the predictive coding to rigorous sampling and testing for quality-control purposes, with the knowledge that expert testimony would likely be needed to explain how well the approach actually worked. Although such showings of reasonableness in the underlying methodology and the specific application might not require the formality of a *Daubert*-type hearing under FRE 702,[26] the litigant would nevertheless have to be prepared for a vigorous defense of predictive coding.

The anticipated use of the technology should be disclosed to the opposing party at the very outset, presumably part of negotiations for a proposed discovery plan under FRCP 26. There is, of course, a strong possibility that discovery will never take place or that, if it does, no document demand of the type that would lend itself to predictive coding will be made. But if that turns out to be true, the groundwork would have already been laid for restarting the demonstration in another suitable case.

Should the use of predictive coding be challenged by an opposing party, either at the time the discovery plan was submitted or after the production was made, an opportunity would then present itself for seeking judicial acknowledgment that this specific use of predictive coding appeared to be a reasonable method to ensure that the production was in compliance with FRCP 26(g)(1)(B) while minimizing inadvertent disclosures. A favorable decision as a result of a hearing on the matter would almost certainly not come in the form of a blanket

---

[26] A formal hearing under *Daubert v. Merrell Dow Pharm., Inc.*, 509 U.S. 579 (1993), held for the purpose of assessing the reliability of expert testimony, might consider whether a scientific theory or technique has been tested, whether it has been subjected to peer review, whether it has been published, what the known or potential error rates might be, what standards control its operation, and whether it has attracted widespread acceptance within the relevant scientific community. It is not entirely clear whether a decision regarding the appropriateness of a technological approach for conducting review would require consideration of a similarly detailed set of factors. Compare *Equity Analytics, LLC v. Lundin*, 248 F.R.D. at 333 ("determining whether a particular search methodology . . . will or will not be effective . . . requires expert testimony that meets the requirements of Rule 702 of the Federal Rules of Evidence.") with Peck, 2011 ("I do not think *Daubert* applies").

endorsement of predictive coding; at best, the judge might note that the approach was a reasonable one in light of the particular facts of the case at hand and the arguments advanced by the responding party. Although this result appears to have occurred in *Da Silva Moore*, the lack of finality in that case's discovery process means that the question of reasonableness has not yet been truly addressed in any definitive manner.

Even a negative outcome might act to spur the use of predictive coding because, for the first time, there would be documentation of the specific concerns a judicial officer might have with the technology in a real-life setting, thus setting the stage for a revised (and presumably improved) strategy for seeking approval in a subsequent case. It should be remembered that judicial decisions questioning the use of keyword searches or linear review have not been held out as evidence that either practice is fatally defective, only that the producing party in that specific case failed to advance a convincing argument for the steps it took.

Given the financial and reputational investment required, it would obviously behoove the organizational litigant to carefully choose the venue for this demonstration.[27] One possibility might be the Seventh Circuit, where an Electronic Discovery Pilot Program Committee composed of judges and members of the bar have created a proposed standing order for use by more than three dozen judges participating in an ongoing pilot program designed to test whether the order might help in reducing the costs and burdens of e-discovery.[28] One principle outlined in the proposed order notes that one of the topics that should be discussed by the parties at an FRCP 26(f) conference include not only keyword searching but also "mathematical or thesaurus-based topic or concept clustering, or other advanced culling technologies."[29] Another option might be to select cases in courthouses in which there is a good chance that the judge overseeing the matter is one who has considered such issues in the past, who is well versed in the nuances of advanced technological approaches to review, or who has noted in the past that linear review or keyword searches can be flawed or expensive.[30]

Why not take another approach and use the rule-making process to seek more-certain authority for litigants to employ advanced strategies? One problem with this strategy is that, even under the best of circumstances, amending the rules of civil procedure is a glacial process, requiring years of comment and debate. A delay of two or three years would mean that thousands more high-volume production cases will move through the pretrial process without the option of using currently available techniques that might be able to save litigants many millions of dollars in the aggregate. Another problem with this approach is that rule changes may not be the best platform for addressing specific types of technology in any detail, given the likelihood that such technology will evolve quickly into new forms, making the present terminology obsolete. Finally, the three-year experience with FRE 502(b) suggests that even relatively clear pronouncements in the rules and associated comments of the drafters are simply

[27] We are not advocating "forum shopping" in its usual sense because a responding party may have little control over where the case is filed. But the large organizational litigants that we urge to openly employ predictive coding–like processes are likely to be involved in numerous cases in jurisdictions across the country at any single moment. Their decision to use a computer-categorization approach would likely be made for a case already in a court where it is felt that the concept would find a receptive ear.

[28] See Seventh Circuit Electronic Discovery Pilot Program Committee, 2010, 2011.

[29] See Principle 2.05 in "[Proposed] Standing Order Relating to the Discovery of Electronically Stored Information," Seventh Circuit Electronic Discovery Pilot Program Committee, 2011, p. 7.

[30] See, e.g., Peck, 2011.

not enough to overcome the aversion of many lawyers to be, as one of our interviewees put it colorfully, "the first monkey launched into space."

There are other options for advancing the agenda, such as holding a large-scale conference of judges, academics, and vendors to discuss empirical evidence related to predictive coding, or creating independent certification bodies to create standards for predictive applications and audit compliance.[31] These activities would certainly be helpful, but no alternative approach would be more effective than a series of definitive judicial decisions in various federal district courts in moving the legal community toward a general acceptance of computer-categorized review techniques.[32] As discussed previously, there were indications in early 2012 that two cases may be moving in that direction. However, as this monograph went to press, discovery was still in progress in both cases. To truly open the doors to more-efficient ways of conducting large-scale reviews in the face of ever-increasing volumes of digital information, litigants that have complained in the past about the high costs of e-discovery will have to take some very bold steps.

---

[31] See, e.g., Baron, 2011, p. 32; Oard, Baron, et al., 2010, pp. 381–382.

[32] Such decisions and orders of a federal district judge are not binding precedent even on other judges within the same district, but the ruling would very likely receive immediate and widely circulated attention in the legal press.

CHAPTER SEVEN

The Challenges of Preservation

In our initial interviews about production costs, we often heard concerns about the challenges of preserving electronic information long before a demand for production was received. These concerns went well beyond the cases included in our study: They extended to litigation that never reached the discovery stage and even to situations in which no complaint was ever filed. In fact, some in-house counsel expressed more concern about the challenges and costs of preservation than about the costs of responding to requests for document production.

To understand these issues, we conducted a separate set of interviews that focused on these questions:

- How do the costs of preservation within an organization generally compare with costs associated with production?
- How does preservation compare with production in terms of the difficulties involved, the state of controlling authority, the degree to which the process has become routinized and incorporated into the normal course of business, and the organization's "comfort level" when facing these e-discovery challenges?
- What methodological issues would be faced in a rigorous attempt to quantify preservation costs in future research?

The observations that emerged from these interviews, which we set forth in this chapter, paint a useful picture of how preservation should be viewed within the context of e-discovery. They also have important policy implications, as we explain at the end of the chapter.

Barriers to Collecting Preservation Cost Data

Most interviewees did not hesitate to confess that their preservation costs had not been systematically tracked in any way and that they were unclear as to how such tracking might be accomplished, though collecting useful metrics was generally asserted as an important future goal for the company.

Part of the reason for a lack of existing information in this area appears to be that much of preservation involves expenditures incurred internally, such as the costs of IT staff time, law department attorney and paralegal time, other employees' time (such as the effort required of custodians to comply with legal-hold notices), and purchases and licensing of applications and hardware to handle preservation. There are exceptions to this internal orientation of preservation expenses, such as when backup tapes are warehoused at a secure facility, when vendors are used for forensic imaging of large numbers of hard drives, or when the advice of outside counsel is sought for drafting the proper language to be used in legal-hold notices. For the most part, however, preservation triggers primarily internal costs, which, as discussed previously, appear to be the least tracked source of e-discovery expenditures. Even in the small fraction of U.S. corporations that require in-house counsel to record time expenditures at the litigation level, efforts expended for preserving data generally may not always be a type of service or event covered by the task or matter codes available in the timekeeping system. Presumably, timekeeping for preservation efforts expended by other employees in an organization, such as those made by record-management staff or IT support, would have similar shortcomings.

In addition, preservation responsibilities can sometimes involve enterprise-level costs, such as would be incurred with the implementation of an automatic legal-hold tool. Such applications are certainly costly and have an observable price tag, but the expenditures are spread across all of the company's present and future preservation needs. Some aspects of preservation may also be intertwined with other business purposes, such as regulatory compliance or record management, which may work against easily identifying those activities associated only with legal processes.

Finally, definitional issues come into play. The scope of what might constitute an expense associated with preservation is not subject to uniform interpretation. Although few would challenge an approach that included time spent issuing a legal-hold notice in any calculation of preservation costs, it is less clear whether the indirect effects on business productivity should be included as well. For example, there may be economic impacts resulting from a decision not to adopt certain IT products (such as instant messaging or social-networking platforms) that might present significant difficulties when preserving information, from not implementing more-efficient data systems due to the need to maintain older legacy platforms and processes, from slower computer-system performance caused by halting the routine deletion of obsolete information in transactional databases, or from a reduced ability to recover lost but nevertheless important data due to a shift from a long-term data backup process to a short-term disaster-recovery system primarily because of preservation concerns. This uncertainty associated with defining the type of costs clearly associated with preservation, along with the obvious difficulty in calculating what such indirect costs might be, appears to be an additional factor discouraging self-collected metrics in this area.

These reported difficulties in collecting usable information regarding preservation expenses are not unique to the companies we contacted. Despite the costs of preservation having become one of the most discussed topics in the legal press of late, we are not aware of *any* empirical research that has collected quantitative information about such costs across significant numbers of actual cases.[1] Our assumption is that the reasons for the dearth of scholarship here are more methodological than any reflection of a lack of interest in the subject.

One large-scale, comprehensive study of discovery costs, for example, asked more than 2,000 attorneys connected with a sample of federal cases terminating in late 2008 whether their clients had implemented legal holds. About half of the attorneys representing parties responding to discovery requests in those cases reported that a hold had been initiated, and

[1] At the time of this writing, we were informed that a survey of preservation costs in large companies was in the planning stages, with the goal of producing a report in 2012 describing preservation-related expenditures for internal staff, outside counsel, IT infrastructure, "diversion of resources from non-legal functions," and "risk and uncertainty of legal rules governing preservation" (Hubbard, 2011, pp. 11–14).

another quarter indicated that there were no holds, but 26 percent of the attorneys could not or would not say one way or another.[2] Presumably, the response rate would have been much lower if the focus had been on the size of expenditures associated with such legal holds instead of simply asking the relatively straightforward question of whether a hold had been in place. It is also telling that, of the more than 80 questions included in the survey—one primarily designed to shed some sorely needed light on e-discovery costs—only the question described above directly touched on preservation. The experienced researchers who led this study have pointed out elsewhere that "preservation duties with respect to ESI" are among the "particularly knotty issues" of pretrial discovery and have called for "additional, credible research on the relationship between pretrial discovery and litigation costs."[3] It is therefore reasonable to assume that the absence of more-focused questions on preservation costs in their large-scale, case-based survey reflected a lack of confidence that reliable information could be collected in such a manner.

Our interviews suggest that this situation may change in the near future. Most organizational litigants with whose representatives we spoke acknowledged a need to do a better job of measuring their preservation costs. One reason they cited was the need to improve the efficiency and effectiveness of the company's overall approach to preservation duties. Quality metrics would, it was said, help in making important decisions about whether to invest in expensive enterprise-level legal-hold tools.[4] Another reason is that companies are eager to present a more persuasive argument to the court when challenging what are believed to be unusual, disproportional, or overly broad preservation demands. But though ongoing efforts by the EDRM group to develop standardized metrics for the preservation process may assist organizations in achieving these goals, the information gap in this area is currently substantial.[5]

Differences in Views of Relative Costs of Preservation and Production

Despite the considerable difficulties currently faced in collecting case-level *quantitative* data regarding preservation expenses, *qualitative* data can help to paint a useful picture of how preservation should be viewed against the backdrop of e-discovery in general. We asked interviewees for their opinions of how overall preservation costs compare with overall costs associated with production within their organizations. The focus here was not individual cases; instead, we were interested in total costs across all of the company's discovery efforts. The specific frame

---

[2] Lee and Willging, 2009, pp. 21–22.

[3] Lee and Willging, 2010, p. 787.

[4] For example, one of the participants in our data collection described the company's recent acquisition of a legal-hold–compliance system. Although the original idea of doing so seemed to be a good one in light of what were believed to be unreasonably large costs for preservation-related tasks, the lack of "firm figures" for past expenditures meant that the decision constituted what was described as a "leap of faith," increasing the difficulties of getting "buy-in" from the "business folks" who had to approve the purchase. Although the interviewee's current perception is that the system has helped reduce preservation expenses to "minimal" levels, the representative was unable to state with certainty whether there have been any actual cost savings.

[5] The current edition of the EDRM code set for preservation-related metrics seeks to describe, in terms of costs, count, volume, and time, the identified custodians; the systems in which ESI reside, as well as the data's formats, purpose, and media types; the quality-assurance and quality-control tasks undertaken; and the specific activities performed to preserve the information (EDRM, undated [b]).

of reference (such as average annual costs or costs incurred within the recent past) was up to the interviewees. We chose to frame our question in this way because we felt that it would be reasonable to assume that key personnel tasked with overseeing e-discovery activities in these companies would be in a unique position to consider, for example, how the level of effort spent by IT department staff for preservation duties over the course of a year compares with the effort they spent for other e-discovery tasks during the same period, how application and hardware purchases compare, how vendor service expenditures compare, or how outside counsel billings compare, even if they would be unable to state with certainty what the totals might have been in any individual case. Until better metrics are developed and routinely utilized by litigants, such opinions constitute the best source currently available for understanding the relative costs of preservation and production, at least in the organizations participating in this study.

For some participants, overall preservation expenses, at least at the time we had these discussions, were strongly felt to overwhelm production-cycle costs. But for others, litigation-related expenses for collection, processing, and especially review in live litigation consistently dominated their total e-discovery spend. Understanding why a company representative's opinion might fall into one group or another can provide insight into the ways organizations approach preservation challenges.

In companies in which preservation costs were reported as predominating, there were several reasons offered for the representatives' perceptions:

- *Preservation's impact on staff throughout the organization*, especially when individual employees under legal holds have to change how they manage information, such as spending time on daily basis to figure out what data within their environment and control should be retained and what could be deleted or modified.
- Another reason involved significant preservation costs that were continuing to be incurred as a result of *long-term or widespread litigation exposure or ongoing investigations*. These costs might arise, for example, from the continued storage of thousands of backup tapes taken off-line years ago or from the need to replace considerable numbers of otherwise business-ready computers that had been physically secured in anticipation of possible requests for forensic investigations. Long-term exposure also was said to increase the need to maintain an expensive capability to preserve data in now-unused legacy systems. The storage requirements of data preserved at any one point in time were also asserted as tipping the balance toward preservation as the primary source of e-discovery expenditures. The purchase price of individual servers needed to store preserved data may not be impressive in and of itself, it was said, but, when associated expenses for network connections, maintenance, redundancy, development, security, and backup are factored in, all resources associated with a single terabyte of preserved data were said to cost in excess of $100,000. One company reported that one-third of its IT department's email resources were now dedicated to preserved information.
- The burdens associated with *implementing and auditing legal holds* in an organization of considerable size and technological complexity were said to generate ongoing expenditures, with staff dedicated to little other than managing preservation chores; such personnel costs were in addition to recent or anticipated multimillion-dollar outlays for centralized legal-hold applications that were hoped to provide a defensible way of documenting their preservation responses.

In companies in which production was said to incur greater expenses than preservation, one or more of four reasons were generally offered:

- *Investments in collection reduced costs of preservation.* In some instances, the company reportedly reaped benefits from investing in an enterprise-level collection tool that was also able to perform a parallel function as a means of routinely preserving data. The company's standard approach was to go out and collect from identified custodians when litigation was initially anticipated or under way, rather than first preserving ESI then waiting for a formal demand for production before collecting. In such instances, the costs of preservation are essentially indistinguishable from the costs of collection.
- *Preservation was nearly always associated with discovery.* Some companies' experiences with preservation were almost always followed up by production of electronic information in large cases that were discovery-heavy and rarely settled. There were few instances in which preservation efforts were triggered by threats of litigation that never actually materialized or by lawsuits in which discovery was never conducted. Here, the significant total costs of production, especially those for review, were larger than the cost of preserving the data at the outset of the same case.
- *Modernizing processes reduces preservation expenditures.* Some companies had worked hard to eliminate operations that created significant preservation costs. For example, traditional practices of retaining many months' worth of backup data had been abandoned in favor of a disaster-recovery system covering a time span too short to be of use in any litigation, the volume of data under sole control of individual employees had been curtailed, a significant investment had been made into more-economical data storage, and steps had been taken to eliminate the need to include outside counsel in most routine preservation activities.
- *Practices were modified such that preservation became the norm.* Some companies had undergone a sea change from a philosophy of "when in doubt, throw it out" to a "retain-everything" policy, at least for those business units with heavy litigation pressure. These companies felt that they were able to incorporate routine preservation processes into their regular course of business, providing opportunities for efficiencies that reduced total preservation expenditures over the long run (and avoided "reacting like [they're in] a fire drill" each time or making forensic copies of the computing resources used by the same custodians over and over again). The companies admitted, however, that the up-front and ongoing costs to place most information produced by their employees into a permanent archiving solution were "enormous."

No matter how a company's representative arrived at his or her opinion of relative costs, all participants reported that expenses associated with preservation now constitute a significant portion of all of the company's discovery-related activities.[6] We certainly were made aware of numerous instances in which a company's specific decision in regard to preservation duties

[6] An informal survey of the members of a group with the stated mission of developing "principles and best practice recommendations for electronic document retention and production in civil litigation" suggested that the "time and effort" expended to identify "potentially discoverable information to comply with preservation" and to store such "information in order to comply with preservation obligations" constituted about 19 percent of the total for both preservation and production (Sedona Conference, 2011, p. 4). It is unclear, however, what percentage of respondents answering this question were in a position to assess the full extent of internal expenditures for preservation.

resulted in surprisingly large expenditures, at least in an absolute sense. Whether those expenditures were unreasonable in light of the stakes of the case is unclear, but the reports do suggest that preservation can require significant outlays of human and financial capital.

Uncertainty Surrounding Preservation Duties

What was an essentially unanimous takeaway from all participants in our interviews was that the level of uncertainty associated with crafting a proper and appropriate preservation response was uncomfortably high at times, especially in light of rapidly shifting winds in controlling authority.

In contrast, there was little concern voiced about problems in identifying the point at which the duty to preserve is actually triggered. Participants appeared to be confident that the warning signs suggesting a reasonable likelihood of future litigation or regulatory investigation would be fairly obvious to experienced counsel. It should be noted that one interviewee at a company with a particularly aggressive preservation strategy remarked that, if the trigger point were restricted to the actual receipt of a complaint or subpoena, there would be a greatly reduced need for the organization to make the effort to archive essentially every business-related document or communication as it does now. But, in general, determining when a duty to preserve has arisen was not reported to be a problem for our participating organizations.

Although the onset of the duty might be obvious in most instances, company contacts indicated it was not always equally clear that the specific preservation choices they have made in the past or were currently making were defensible ones. This lack of certainty was asserted to result in organizations casting a "preservation net" that was either wider (e.g., inclusion of custodians or data locations with questionable connections to the facts of the litigation) or with a finer mesh (e.g., securing entire drives rather than individual active files) than what might have been utilized had they been more confident about their choices, especially when compared with the amount of information subsequently collected from the preserved data. A commonly voiced fear was that, despite good-faith efforts to comply with the current state of the law, the scope of what was preserved or the specific process chosen to implement preservation might subsequently be determined as inadequate. The potentially catastrophic ramifications of such a finding in terms of money, case outcomes, or professional reputations were said to require erring heavily on the side of caution.

There were two distinct cost-related issues that arose during our discussions about the scope and process of preservation: (1) the potential for overpreservation and (2) the awareness that compliance could never be fail-safe. The first involved ongoing concerns that not enough custodians or data might be included in their efforts to prevent inadvertent destruction or modification of ESI. An example was given in which 100 custodians were placed on legal holds even though it was never likely that data would be collected from more than five. "Never likely" was said be an insufficient assurance of negligible risk, so it was claimed that there would be unnecessary costs incurred as a result of imposing 95 other holds without any meaningful benefit in the resolution of the dispute in question. Such assertions are not unlike those made by some stakeholders who advocate for health care liability reform. Their claims that expensive and unnecessary overtesting is routinely performed in the face of uncertain risk and exposure arising out of potential medical malpractice litigation were echoed by what we heard from companies participating in this study, even from those who believed that they had taken significant steps to minimize preservation expenditures. With few reliable benchmarks currently available for assessing the risk of employing a particular preservation strategy in each case or dispute they face, company representatives felt that the most prudent approach was to go beyond a relatively conservative assessment of custodians, data locations, and data types with potentially relevant evidence and markedly expand the volume of information subject to preservation.

Such concerns about the costs associated with overpreservation appeared to be related primarily to what were asserted to be unnecessary expenditures to lock down and store the information (e.g., the value of time spent by IT staff to mirror hard drives or the capital investment required to create adequate server capacity for preserved files). Costs arising from a corresponding need to perform collection and processing tasks on a much larger universe of data than might have been preserved under a different legal environment were not a commonly mentioned complaint.

The second cost issue involved the choices that needed to be made in order to create a preservation process that was as thorough as practically possible. It was asserted that no matter how much effort might be invested into crafting a comprehensive preservation plan, the reality is that something minor will often go wrong. Human error, a notice to preserve being overlooked or lost in the email system, a folder missed, a hard drive not inventoried—all are events that were said to have an excellent chance of occurring in organizations of the size and scope included in this study.

It was not clear to most of the representatives with whom we spoke what the ramifications of such inadvertent mistakes might be. This was less of an issue of direct costs for preservation (though one participant suggested that additional steps taken by his company to reduce the chance for error to a minimum had significant economic implications) than about the potential for a downstream hit for monetary sanctions, adverse-inference instructions, or some other undesirable and presumably costly outcome. Much of the discussion in this regard focused on the process of imposing a legal hold within the organization and making sure that employees followed both the intent and letter of the directives to preserve. Corporations with widely distributed computing assets in which control over individual files were primarily in the hands of the individual employees who created them appeared to have the greatest concerns in this area. Crafting a preservation approach that defensibly balanced the risks of giving those same employees the primary responsibility to safeguard ESI under their immediate control against the much greater costs of tasking IT or security personnel with the duty of directly seizing the data was said to be particularly difficult. An organizational litigant might believe that the steps it took were reasonable and in proportion to the stakes of the litigation and the value of the information. However, it was asserted, there are few guarantees that a judge would see the reasonability and proportionality in the same way.

It should be noted that we perceived a greater comfort level regarding the preservation process in those companies that had completed the installation of an automated legal-hold–compliance system (some other participants were in the process of implementing such a system or seriously considering the purchase of one, but, at the time we spoke, these were future goals). The manner in which these hold applications operate varies, but one commonly employed application initially notifies a custodian by email that he or she has been placed on a legal hold. Once the custodian opens that email, he or she is required to acknowledge receipt of the notification of legal hold, having read it, and understanding what he or she is obligated to do. The notice provides the custodian with the names and contact information for the key attorneys overseeing the case, the name of the dispute, the subject matter, and a description of the data sources and types requested to be protected from deletion or modification. In addition, managers in the IT department receive a similar notification, one that requires them to take direct steps, such as suspending any routine document-destruction processes for the custodians in question or securing computing resources should the employees leave the company or upgrade their computers. Follow-up notices and requests for acknowledgment are distributed to both custodians and managers on a regular basis, and failures to affirm that requests have been received and understood are reported to the attorneys handling the matter and the custodians' managers. The custodians themselves can review the notices and additional instructions for all active holds that affect them. They may also be prompted to respond to questionnaires that seek information about the data under their control or what other custodians or data locations should be included. But it was noted that these automatic compliance systems essentially routinize only the notification and tracking aspects of legal holds; they do not necessarily directly preserve or collect the information in question (though some tools do offer a form of this capability), nor do they confirm that the information under the control of a custodian is secure from inadvertent or intentional modification or deletion.[7] Nevertheless, moving from an ad hoc response for legal holds that depends on individual attorneys to craft and manage both notice and compliance to a process that was more routinized and more consistently documented and auditable was felt to remove some of the danger that the approach would be challenged in the future. But even if the *process* had been improved, there was still uncertainty about the *scope* of preservation. Concerns regarding overpreservation remained important issues even for companies with automated approaches to issuing legal holds.

Interestingly, this level of uncertainty was suggested by one participant as being most acute in the context of governmental investigations. It was not that there were more-stringent requirements for complying with preservation duties in regulatory actions but that the potential downside risks for loss or corruption of ESI were far more serious, including catastrophic disruption of business activities and proposed ventures and even jail time.

An Absence of Clear Legal Authority

If there was one consistent theme in what we heard, it revolved around complaints of a lack of understandable legal authority and guidance that could be comfortably relied on when making preservation decisions. Despite the much-discussed risks of a less-than-comprehensive preservation hold or of a failure to adequately guarantee compliance, there are, in fact, few appellate court opinions that speak directly to the mechanics of preserving ESI. At the moment, the most–widely circulated decisions come from individual federal district court judges and magistrates and therefore cannot be relied on to control the law applied in the many jurisdictions in which the large organizational litigants in our study can find themselves. Such decisions may be influential, but there are no guarantees that a trial court judge in another part of the country will see the same issues in the same way (indeed, the decisions and orders of a federal district judge are not binding precedent in other judicial districts or, as a practical matter, even on different judges within the same district).

[7] For an extensive discussion of the current technological limitations of automated approaches to preservation, see Allman, Baron, and Grossman, 2011.

Examples of conflicting holdings across and within jurisdictions include issues related to whether failure to issue a written legal-hold notice constitutes gross negligence per se,[8] what preservation-related duties exist regarding potentially relevant evidence in the hands of third parties,[9] whether a proportionality standard should be applied in deciding what information to retain,[10] whether spoliation sanctions require a showing of negligence or a more stringent bad-faith standard,[11] or whether sanctions should be imposed for the failure to properly preserve data without any need to show that the lost information was relevant or helpful to the requesting party.[12] As a result, preservation practices applied to computer resources located at a company's central office may be subject to very different standards when scrutinized by courts in various federal districts and states. When facing this Balkanized authority, interviewees asserted, rational litigants would have few options available other than conforming to rulings that impose the broadest and harshest (at least from a producing party's perspective) preservation duties.

This uncertainty about the scope of preservation duties arising out of a lack of uniform, transjurisdictional policies is exacerbated by what was described as less-than-helpful language and confusing directives sometimes found in judicial opinions and court rules that do speak to preservation issues. Complaints from lawyers and litigants regarding controlling authority that they believe was crafted to provide the widest flexibility to trial judges and appellate justices—thus lending itself to fluid interpretations and uncertainty about the most-appropriate steps to take in response—are certainly not unknown in many other aspects of the civil and criminal justice systems. But, in the context of preservation, a world in which IT, corporate policies, and

---

[8] Compare *Pension Committee of University of Montreal Pension Plan v. Banc of America Securities LLC*, 685 F. Supp. 2d 456 (S.D.N.Y. 2010) ("the failure to issue a *written* litigation hold constitutes gross negligence because that failure is likely to result in the destruction of relevant information") with *Steuben Foods, Inc. v. Country Gourmet Foods, LLC*, 2011 WL 1549450 (W.D.N.Y. Apr. 21, 2011) ("Nor will the court find that the failure to issue a written litigation hold justifies even a rebuttable presumption that spoliation has taken place").

[9] Compare *Velez v. Marriott PR Management, Inc.*, 590 F. Supp. 2d 235 (D.P.R. 2008) ("The duty extends to giving notice if the evidence is in the hands of third-parties") with *Paluch v. Dawson*, 2009 WL 3287395 (M.D. Pa. Oct. 13, 2009) ("As other courts within the Third Circuit have observed, relevant authority requires that . . . the evidence in question must be within the party's control").

[10] Compare *Rimkus Consulting Group, Inc. v. Cammarata*, 688 F. Supp. 2d 598 (S.D. Tex. 2010) ("Whether preservation or discovery conduct is acceptable in a case depends on what is *reasonable*, and that in turn depends on whether what was done—or not done—was *proportional* to that case and consistent with clearly established applicable standards") with *Orbit One Communications, Inc. v. Numerex Corp.*, 271 F.R.D. 429 (S.D.N.Y. 2010) ("Although some cases have suggested that the definition of what must be preserved should be guided by principles of "reasonableness and proportionality," ...this standard may prove too amorphous to provide much comfort to a party deciding what files it may delete or backup tapes it may recycle. Until a more precise definition is created by rule, a party is well-advised to "retain all relevant documents (but not multiple identical copies) in existence at the time the duty to preserve attaches.").

[11] Compare *Velez v. Marriott PR Management, Inc.*, 590 F. Supp. 2d 235 (D.P.R. 2008) ("Applicable caselaw in the First Circuit has clearly established that 'bad faith or comparable bad motive' is not required for the court to exclude evidence in situations involving spoliation.") with *Rimkus Consulting Group, Inc. v. Cammarata*, 688 F. Supp. 2d 598 (S.D. Tex. 2010) ("As a general rule, in this circuit, the severe sanctions of granting default judgment, striking pleadings, or giving adverse inference instructions may not be imposed unless there is evidence of 'bad faith'").

[12] Compare *Pension Comm. of the Univ. of Montreal Pension Plan v. Banc of Am. Sec., LLC*, 685 F. Supp 2d 456 (S.D.N.Y. 2010 ("Relevance and prejudice may be presumed when the spoliating party acted in bad faith or in a grossly negligent manner") with *Orbit One Communs. v. Numerex Corp.*, 271 F.R.D. 429 (S.D.N.Y. 2010) ("a court considering a sanctions motion must make a threshold determination whether any material that has been destroyed was likely relevant even for purposes of discovery").

the law all are rapidly evolving in sometimes-different directions, such complaints may have more traction than is usually the case.

Unlike other aspects of the pretrial process in which litigants' business practices have had many decades to adapt to a rich body of legal authority, the preservation of ESI continues to be perceived as an unfathomable black box, one that seems to require litigants to radically shift gears, as one interviewee put it, whenever the "weekly law bulletins tout some obscure judge's opinion or shout about some new sanction." A key concern revolved around how a company's chosen approach to preservation, which may have seemed reasonable to counsel at the time, might later find itself somewhere on the continuum between total acceptability and serious sanctions.[13] The following comment, which paraphrases the rather hyperbolic analogy offered by one interviewee, captures the frustration of many of those with whom we spoke:

> I know it's negligence not to be paying attention and I wind up running a red light and cause an accident. I know it's gross negligence if I get drunk, run a red light, and cause an accident. And I know it's an intentional or willful act when I deliberately run a red light in order to cause an accident. What I don't know is whether it is negligent, grossly negligent, or intentional misconduct if I don't get a forensic copy of every hard drive in the company each and every time we are sued.

It is important to remember that our focus here is on *litigant perceptions*. Even if one could put forth a convincing argument that, in actual practice, judges across the country essentially speak with one voice when it comes to preservation, the key issue is that repeat litigants (at least the ones with whose representatives we spoke) do not believe that there is an acceptable level of uniformity and certainty in the law when it comes to interpreting what constitutes reasonable scope or reasonable practices. To the extent that litigants regularly act on those beliefs, rightly or wrongly,[14] claims that overpreservation have triggered unnecessary costs may well be justified.

Policy Implication: Need for Guidance

Our primary takeaway from these discussions was the clear and across-the-board desire for standardized, unambiguous, transjurisdictional authority providing guidance for the proper scope of the ESI preservation duty, the manner in which that duty should be discharged, and the types of behavior that would likely be considered sanctionable. Though our original question of whether companies spend more or less on preservation than they do on the production cycle remains of interest, the answer is not likely to be much help to litigants, the courts, or policymakers. A more useful question might be, "Which of these two aspects of e-discovery is the more stable and settled?"

---

[13] For a comprehensive description of how federal circuits differ regarding the law surrounding the imposition of sanctions for preservation shortcomings, see *Victor Stanley, Inc. v. Creative Pipe, Inc.*, 296 F.R.D. 497 (D. Md. 2010), at 542 and "Appendix A to Memorandum, Order and Recommendation: Spoliation Sanctions by Circuit").

[14] One interviewee suggested that at least some of the uncertainty about preservation is fed by the self-interested claims of vendors that are "[peddling] fear and snake oil" by "cherry picking" "little one-off" trial court decisions and give them "outsized play."

A good argument can be made that, in the case of the production cycle, there is far more balance between the state of the law and the state of the technology than ever before. Issues regarding reasonable accessibility in collection, once the primary focus of both the rule-making process and IT system developers, seems to have reached a point of relative stability, with collection having evolved into what might be characterized as a fairly industrialized process in which litigants are generally comfortable with the choices they make. Although we argue elsewhere in this monograph that affirmative steps are needed to encourage the increased use of computerized approaches to help reduce the considerable costs of examining electronic documents for relevance, responsiveness, or privilege, the organizational litigants we contacted reported few uncertainties about what the law requires of them when it comes to review. Regarding preservation, however, a similar understanding between litigant practices and controlling authority does not appear to have been reached.

The exact nature and form for such guidance is beyond the scope of this monograph.[15] We collected no data, quantitative or qualitative, that we believe would help shape the specific language of rules addressing ESI preservation. But it is clear that, of the e-discovery areas we examined in this study, preservation is the one most in need of concerted action on the part of the policymaking community.

---

[15] Indeed, there have been arguments advanced that rule proposals dealing with preservation issues may run afoul of the Rules Enabling Act (see 28 U.S.C. § 2072) because they could go beyond prescribing general rules of practice and procedure and rules of evidence for cases as authorized by the act, given that preservation rules may regulate conduct never associated with actual litigation. See, e.g., West, 2011, p. 3. But see Allman, 2010, pp. 222–224:

> The test of Enabling Act jurisdiction, or, for that matter, the use of inherent judicial power, is the relationship of the conduct to be regulated to the functioning of the courts. The mere fact that an action has not yet been commenced is not decisive.

Another argument against relying solely on uniform federal preservation authority is that the duty generally lies in state law, so federal solutions that would define both the duty and when sanctions are appropriate may not displace state law in federal cases brought under diversity jurisdiction (federal courts are permitted to hear cases involving citizens of different states, even if questions of federal law are not raised; in such instances, federal court rules apply to the process and state laws apply to the substantive legal questions). See generally Vail, 2011.

Finally, preservation rulemaking may conflict with existing requirements regarding the destruction, alteration, or falsification of records subject to regulatory investigations or administration. See, e.g., West, 2011, pp. 4–5.

CHAPTER EIGHT

Conclusions and Recommendations

It will come as no surprise to experienced litigants that the costs associated with large-scale document reviews dominate total production expenditures—$0.73 of every dollar spent on electronic production in our set of 57 cases was spent on review. As the volume of digital information grows every year, the problem becomes more urgent: How can the costs of review be addressed?

We found little room for improvement in these costs if litigants continue to use linear processes that require eyes-on inspection of every document. The costs of attorney services in the United States for large-scale reviews, if current practices continue, are unlikely to drop to a point at which the overall costs of review would be reduced to levels similar to those seen for processing or collection tasks. Though less expensive reviewers can be found offshore, that option may not be viable ones for many litigants. The rates at which humans are able to read documents and make thoughtful legal decisions are likely to have reached their upper bound as well, despite the use of creative technologies that help better organize documents for review. Such realities need to be viewed in light of the fact that traditional eyes-on review approaches are far from error-free, with considerable empirical evidence that troubling proportions of the decisions made in large-scale reviews would be overruled by other reviewers with similar training and experience.

The most promising alternative available today for large-scale reviews is the use of predictive coding and other computerized categorization strategies that can rank electronic documents by the likelihood that they are relevant, responsive, or privileged. Eyes-on review is still required but only for a much smaller set of documents determined to be the most-likely candidates for production. Empirical research suggests that predictive coding is at least as accurate as humans in traditional large-scale review. Moreover, there is evidence that the number of hours of attorney time that would be required in a large-scale review could be reduced by as much as three-fourths, depending on the nature of the documents and other factors, which would make predictive coding one answer to the critical need of significantly reducing review costs. It is certainly not the sole answer, and any cost savings may be negligible unless litigants first take a holistic approach to controlling expenditures from the initial signs of impending litigation through final data delivery, including reaching out to demanding parties at an early point in a spirit of cooperation and collaboration. But, assuming that best practices have been followed throughout the e-discovery life cycle, these new techniques may be the most practical way for litigants to markedly reduce costs associated with the most expensive component of ESI production.[1]

Despite the apparent promise of predictive coding and other computerized categorization techniques, however, the legal world has been reluctant to embrace the new technology. There are many reasons for this reluctance, including concerns regarding under- or overinclusion of responsive documents, the ability of computerized review to identify privileged or sensitive communications, and the resistance of outside counsel to move away from an important part of their practice, but the key reason is the absence of widespread judicial approval of the methodology, specifically regarding any acknowledgment of the adequacy of the results in actual cases or whether the process was a reasonable way to prevent inadvertent privilege waiver. Without clear signs from the bench that the use of computer-categorized review tools should be considered in the same light as eyes-on review or keyword searching, litigants involved in large-scale reviews are unlikely to employ the technologies on a routine basis.

It should be noted that our conclusions about the most obvious way to reduce overall production expenditures are no doubt shaped by the cases we included in our analysis. Our data collection was one that focused on what could be characterized as large-scale discovery productions, events that FJC research has suggested take place in only a fraction of all federal litigation. It may well be true that, when pretrial discovery involves more-modest volumes, the costs of review do not play as large of a role in driving total expenditures. Tasks involving collection or processing could conceivably present a greater cost burden for the producing parties when volumes are smaller. Moreover, computer applications for conducting review are unlikely to be economically viable options when dealing with smaller document sets, in which any savings in attorney hours might be overwhelmed by vendor costs and machine-training requirements. Existing approaches, such as deduplication, cluster analysis, and email threading, may provide a more practical answer in these situations. In addition, the organizations that participated in the study, some of the largest corporations in the United States, can arguably be thought of as relatively sophisticated litigants when it comes to e-discovery. Our interviews revealed that they have already taken significant steps to address many technological and logistical issues associated with pretrial discovery of ESI, steps that may be beyond the financial capabilities and available internal resources of smaller or less experienced organizations.

Our conversations with litigants about preservation revealed that this task had evolved into a significant portion of their companies' total e-discovery expenditures. Some of the companies in our study believed that preserving information was now costing them more in the aggregate than producing e-discovery, although all interviewees admitted that their companies do not systematically track preservation costs. The way in which organizations perceive such costs appears to be related to steps taken (or not taken) to move away from ad hoc preserva-

[1] The question of whether costs could be reduced significantly through more-effective case management by the judge supervising the litigation, such as employing various techniques for narrowing discovery or requiring discovery to proceed in phases, is not considered in this monograph. Nor did we explore whether cooperative discovery agreements between opposing parties could routinely result in slashing pretrial litigation costs for both sides. And the use (or, in actual practice, the lack of use) of "clawback" or "quick-peek" arrangements under the provisions of FRE 502 to reduce or eliminate the need for privilege review was not considered (note that such FRE 502 agreements would have little impact on the need to review for relevant and responsie documents, presumably the most costly component of traditional review). None of these avenues for reducing litigant expenditures is without merit, and each deserves focused, empirical investigation to accurately describe how often it is currently employed and its potential for cost savings. We do remain convinced that computer-categorized document review applications offer the most immediate promise for significantly reducing costs in large-scale productions.

tion strategies, the nature of their caseloads, and ongoing impacts on computing services and business practices.

The most common theme we heard during our interviews involved litigant uncertainty about what strategies are adequate for preservation. Determining the reasonable scope for a legal hold in terms of custodians, data locations, and volume was said to be a murky process at best, with strong incentives to overpreserve in the face of the risk for significant sanctions if any potentially relevant data are advertently altered or destroyed. Similar concerns were voiced about the process itself, with few concrete guideposts said to be available to provide litigants with a comfortable level of assurance when deciding not only what to preserve, but how.

The cause for such worries is undoubtedly the absence of standardized controlling legal authority in this area. Although some judicial decisions have addressed preservation scope and process, they act as legally binding precedent only in specific jurisdictions or they conflict with decisions rendered by other courts on the same issues. As a result, litigants reported that they were greatly concerned about not making defensible decisions involving preservation and the looming potential of serious sanctions.

Recommendations

To address the costs of e-discovery document production and uncertainty about how best to preserve electronic information, we make the following three recommendations.

Facilitate Predictive Coding to Reduce the Costs of Review

The exponential growth in digital information, which shows no signs of slowing, makes a computer-categorized review strategy, such as predictive coding, not only a cost-effective choice but perhaps the *only* reasonable way to handle many large-scale productions. Despite efforts to cull data down as much as possible in the processing stage of the cycle, review sets in some cases may be impossible to examine thoroughly using humans, at least not in time frames that make sense during ongoing litigation. Predictive coding and similar approaches may be far from the "silver bullets" sometimes touted by their developers and vendors, but clinging to the traditional approaches used for review when litigants and lawyers lived in a paper-based world no longer makes sense.

The use of computerized categorization techniques, such as predictive coding, will likely become the norm for large-scale reviews in the future, given the likelihood of increasing societal acceptance of artificial intelligence technologies that might have seemed like improbable science fiction only a few decades ago. The problem is that considerable sums of money are being spent unnecessarily today while attitudes slowly change over time. New court rules might move the process forward, but the best catalyst for more-widespread use of predictive coding would be well-publicized instances of successful implementation in cases in which the process has received close judicial scrutiny. It will be up to forward-thinking litigants to make that happen.

Improve Tracking of Costs of Preservation and Production

During the course of this research, we were repeatedly struck by the inability of well-regarded corporations operating on an immense scale to provide information about discovery-related expenditures with aggregate values exceeding millions of dollars. In some instances, we met with in-house lawyers who were intimately familiar with the legal nuances and factual backgrounds of the claims and defenses in cases they managed but were at a loss to describe what it cost their employers to collect, process, and review hundreds of gigabytes of data in those same cases. This lack of information might have been understandable during an era when outside counsel were usually in sole charge of the prosecution and defense of lawsuits in which the organization was involved, when great deference was given to such counsel's strategic and operational decisions, and when the organization's primary role was to pay the firm's monthly invoices in a timely manner. As in-house attorneys are quick to point out, however, that model has changed radically in light of new economic realities.

One reason that companies need to track discovery expenditure data involves important choices they will have to make in the years to come. A ceaseless upward movement in the volume of information that businesses will collect in the future is all but an absolute certainty, and much of that information will be discoverable. Ad hoc responses to discovery needs in individual cases might have been reasonable solutions in the past, but the scale of the effort required to comply with the demands of opposing parties has grown markedly in recent years, making more-systematic approaches the only viable options when dealing with massive data volumes. Corporations will need to carefully consider whether it makes sense for them to purchase or license solutions, such as automated legal-hold compliance systems, enterprise-wide collection tools, dedicated servers for storing litigation-related data, or advanced analytical software for early case assessment or in-house document review. Although the costs of acquiring such tools can be spread across a company's litigation portfolio, none of these solutions can be thought of as inexpensive, and convincing the business side of a corporation of such tools' utility can be difficult without solid information to back up the argument. Rational and reasoned choices whether to make these investments, allow vendors or outside counsel to handle such chores, or employ different strategies are possible only if a company has good institutional memory about the all-in costs for discovery in individual cases. Costs are obviously incurred for keeping such detailed records, but the costs of buying products that are not truly needed or of spending months in personnel time doing chores that could more efficiently be handled by computers may well be much greater.

An equally important reason for paying closer attention to discovery expenditures is the need to present a credible argument to a judge that a proposed discovery plan or request would result in unreasonably large expenditures. Back-of-the-envelope calculations for estimating one's discovery costs may be adequate for internal planning, but a court is likely to require a more persuasive level of precision, including the projected costs of alternative approaches for complying with discovery obligations.[2] Moreover, as we have shown, the per-gigabyte costs of production-related tasks vary greatly across cases, making reliance on generalized rules of thumb a risky proposition.[3] Those unit costs are likely to be influenced by a company's unique mix of personnel, technological resources, and standard discovery practices, requiring historical data arising out of the company's own experiences to accurately project costs.

[2] See, for example, *Spieker v. Quest Cherokee, LLC*, 2009 WL 2168892 (D. Kan. July 21, 2009), at *3:

> Clearly, there are multiple approaches to electronic discovery and alternatives for reducing costs and it appears that defendant asserts the highest estimates possible merely to support its argument that electronic discovery is unduly burdensome. Under the circumstances, the court concludes that defendant's estimate of the cost to conduct a 'privilege and relevance' review is greatly exaggerated.

[3] See, e.g., Degnan, 2011.

A lack of detailed information, especially regarding internal expenditures, can also present a misleading, and potentially costly, picture to the court. Most of the cases in our data collection had estimated internal expenditures of less than 10 percent, but there were some that exceeded 25 percent. To the extent that litigants continue to shoulder a greater part of the discovery load directly as they take on additional tasks once farmed out to vendors or handled by outside counsel, projected costs that do not include the effort expended by law department counsel and paralegals, IT staff, and other corporate employees will underestimate the actual burden placed on a litigant from a proposed discovery plan or discovery demand. In instances in which cost shifting is a possibility, the inability to document all costs associated with a production will result in reduced reimbursement.

Finally, the need for better e-discovery metrics may loom largest in the area of preservation. Although we are confident that the costs of review overwhelm those incurred by other tasks in the production cycle, there is considerable uncertainty involved in analyzing the financial impact that preservation can have on organizational litigants, especially in comparison to production costs. If companies are not able to predict or describe such costs with reasonable precision, it will be difficult for them to make reasoned choices in developing legal-hold strategies at the first sign of anticipated litigation. Lack of such information also frustrates rulemaking efforts intended to offer effective solutions to stakeholder complaints.

None of these concerns was lost on the companies participating in this study. Many representatives spoke freely about their desires to better understand discovery-related expenditures, with some describing plans to institute new procedures to track costs for various components of the process. Although following through on those plans will require changes in how internal staff record their time, how outside counsel describe tasks performed for legal services on the company's behalf, and how vendors report on data-processing work and other chores, we strongly urge these and similarly situated organizational litigants to do so.

Develop Transjurisdictional Authority for Preservation

Our research has convinced us that steps must be taken soon to address litigant concerns about preservation. Our interviewees repeatedly touched on concerns about the lack of consistent and detailed legal authority to guide their preservation efforts, resulting in uncertainty about proper scope, defensible processes, and sanctionable behavior. To the extent that this uncertainty begets overpreservation and unnecessary expenses, the continuing growth in the volume of data stored by organizations in the regular course of business suggests that the financial problems associated with preservation will increase as well.

At the time this monograph was written, there were proposals advanced to the federal judiciary's Advisory Committee on Civil Rules that appear to be intended to address at least some of these concerns.[4] Determining whether any of these specific proposals offers an efficient and effective answer to the lack of guidance is beyond the scope of this monograph, but it is clear that the problems noted are unlikely to go away through the traditional evolution of the common law. Without transjurisdictional authority on which to rely, lawyers will continue to find themselves unsure of whether the advice they provide to their organizational clients about IT system architecture and processes will hold up to scrutiny before the judges in whatever courts they might find themselves. The only ways to acquire such cross-border authority would

---

[4] See, e.g., Judicial Conference of the United States, 2010b, as well as documents collected from U.S. Courts, 2011.

be Supreme Court decision, congressional action, or modification of existing rules of court. Of the three avenues, the latter seems to be the most practical.

Next Steps

We noted at the outset of this monograph that our data collection and analysis were narrowly focused. Our primary interests were in the costs borne by responding parties to comply with document demands, in proposing possible avenues for addressing those costs, and in understanding how such costs compared with those for preservation efforts. Such an approach does not, however, include many other important aspects of discovery, such as costs incurred by the demanding parties in acquiring and analyzing ESI, the benefit that the discovery process can have for the resolution of disputes, and the indirect impacts that e-discovery can have on organizations. All are worthy topics of research.

Our hope is that this monograph will help inform the current debate about how to adapt litigant practices and controlling authority to address concerns about the costs of production and preservation. We have been encouraged by the recent actions of the Judicial Conference's Advisory Committee on Civil Rules in bringing together academics, judges, practitioners, vendors, and others to explore discovery-related issues in a manner informed by quantitative and qualitative data. This type of broad-based inquiry is exactly what is needed to take into account the effect that proposed e-discovery policies can have on every aspect of litigants' costs, from initial preservation to final presentation. Focusing on only a few parts of that continuum will likely lead to controlling costs in one area only to have them increase elsewhere.

APPENDIX A

Supplemental Tables

Table A.1
Production Costs per Gigabyte Produced, 33 Cases

Subject Matter	Cost per Gigabyte Produced ($)
Intellectual property	6,675
Antitrust	10,603
Antitrust	11,433
Intellectual property	12,988
Product liability	13,699
Fraud or false claims	13,892
Product liability	14,211
Government subpoena	14,679
Fraud or false claims	17,231
Product liability	18,712
Government subpoena	19,231
Fraud or false claims	21,691
Product liability	22,813
Intellectual property	22,815
Government subpoena	24,578
Product liability	32,850
Intellectual property	36,300
Intellectual property	37,564
Government subpoena	40,176
Intellectual property	47,196
Product liability	52,943
Intellectual property	56,518
Employment	63,087
Contract	80,331

Table A.1—Continued

Subject Matter	Cost per Gigabyte Produced ($)
Intellectual property	138,357
Government subpoena	163,264
Intellectual property	251,091
Government subpoena	251,489
Contract	261,639
Government subpoena	274,409
Fraud or false claims	306,352
Intellectual property	330,532
Intellectual property	906,109

Table A.2
Review Costs per Gigabyte Reviewed, 35 Cases

Subject Matter	Cost per Gigabyte Reviewed ($)
Intellectual property	4,039
Intellectual property	6,425
Antitrust	8,055
Antitrust	8,657
Fraud or false claims	10,990
Fraud or false claims	10,991
Product liability	11,321
Government subpoena	11,842
Intellectual property	11,885
Government subpoena	12,731
Product liability	13,307
Intellectual property	13,337
Product liability	13,559
Government subpoena	15,759
Government subpoena	15,795
Intellectual property	17,624
Contract	18,090
Product liability	18,199
Fraud or false claims	19,116
Product liability	19,403
Intellectual property	19,505

Table A.2—Continued

Subject Matter	Cost per Gigabyte Reviewed ($)
Government subpoena	19,824
Contract	20,770
Intellectual property	21,494
Intellectual property	23,784
Intellectual property	29,566
Intellectual property	30,016
Fraud or false claims	30,326
Employment	33,815
Government subpoena	33,828
Government subpoena	38,557
Product liability	52,943
Intellectual property	74,540
Government subpoena	158,325
Intellectual property	358,439

Table A.3
Collection Costs as a Percentage of All Production Costs, 44 Cases

Subject Matter	Collection Costs as a Percentage of Total Costs
Intellectual property	0.8
Contract	1.0
Contract	1.5
Fraud or false claims	2.0
Product liability	2.0
Government subpoena	2.2
Antitrust	2.7
Product liability	2.7
Government subpoena	3.8
Intellectual property	4.3
Contract	4.3
Government subpoena	4.4
Intellectual property	4.5
Employment	4.9
Product liability	5.3

Table A.3—Continued

Subject Matter	Collection Costs as a Percentage of Total Costs
Intellectual property	5.3
Intellectual property	6.3
Government subpoena	6.5
Fraud or false claims	6.6
Antitrust	6.7
Intellectual property	7.1
Intellectual property	7.4
Fraud or false claims	7.7
Intellectual property	7.9
Intellectual property	8.1
Government subpoena	8.2
Contract	8.5
Product liability	8.8
Government subpoena	9.7
Product liability	10.2
Intellectual property	11.1
Intellectual property	11.4
Product liability	12.7
Government subpoena	13.3
Intellectual property	13.5
Government subpoena	13.7
Fraud or false claims	14.3
Government subpoena	16.5
Government subpoena	20.0
Product liability	23.3
Intellectual property	23.7
Intellectual property	24.0
Intellectual property	24.7
Intellectual property	25.5

Table A.4
Per-Custodian Collection Costs, 35 Cases

Subject Matter	Collection Costs per Custodian ($)
Contract	29
Government subpoena	313
Product liability	409
Intellectual property	464
Fraud or false claims	617
Antitrust	619
Government subpoena	652
Intellectual property	676
Intellectual property	693
Government subpoena	695
Government subpoena	754
Intellectual property	918
Product liability	959
Intellectual property	1,017
Intellectual property	1,227
Contract	1,246
Intellectual property	1,496
Government subpoena	1,536
Employment	1,747
Fraud or false claims	1,757
Intellectual property	1,770
Intellectual property	2,267
Fraud or false claims	2,405
Government subpoena	2,653
Fraud or false claims	3,165
Intellectual property	3,662
Contract	3,718
Product liability	4,339
Government subpoena	4,623
Product liability	4,659
Product liability	5,084
Antitrust	5,607
Intellectual property	5,629

Table A.4—Continued

Subject Matter	Collection Costs per Custodian ($)
Government subpoena	6,146
Government subpoena	6,223

Table A.5
Processing Costs as a Percentage of All Production Costs, 44 Cases

Subject Matter	Processing Costs as a Percentage of Total Costs
Intellectual property	0.0
Product liability	4.4
Product liability	4.7
Contract	4.7
Fraud or false claims	6.3
Product liability	6.3
Government subpoena	7.1
Product liability	7.2
Antitrust	8.5
Product liability	8.5
Contract	10.1
Fraud or false claims	10.5
Intellectual property	11.1
Government subpoena	12.0
Intellectual property	13.6
Intellectual property	13.6
Government subpoena	14.1
Intellectual property	14.1
Employment	15.6
Intellectual property	15.9
Government subpoena	16.7
Product liability	17.9
Intellectual property	19.8
Fraud or false claims	20.9
Antitrust	21.2
Intellectual property	22.6
Government subpoena	22.9

Table A.5—Continued

Subject Matter	Processing Costs as a Percentage of Total Costs
Intellectual property	23.6
Fraud or false claims	24.2
Intellectual property	25.0
Intellectual property	25.4
Intellectual property	25.5
Government subpoena	26.0
Government subpoena	26.3
Contract	26.9
Intellectual property	30.7
Intellectual property	37.2
Product liability	40.1
Intellectual property	40.7
Government subpoena	42.0
Government subpoena	42.2
Intellectual property	42.8
Government subpoena	43.5
Contract	47.7

Table A.6
Review Costs as a Percentage of All Production Costs, 44 Cases

Subject Matter	Review Costs as a Percentage of Total Costs
Intellectual property	37.3
Government subpoena	42.8
Intellectual property	43.7
Government subpoena	44.7
Product liability	47.2
Intellectual property	49.9
Government subpoena	51.2
Contract	51.3
Government subpoena	53.7
Intellectual property	57.9
Intellectual property	58.6

Table A.6—Continued

Subject Matter	Review Costs as a Percentage of Total Costs
Intellectual property	60.1
Government subpoena	60.6
Contract	64.6
Intellectual property	65.2
Government subpoena	65.8
Intellectual property	66.4
Intellectual property	67.1
Fraud or false claims	68.1
Intellectual property	69.0
Intellectual property	70.3
Product liability	71.9
Antitrust	72.0
Product liability	72.1
Fraud or false claims	72.5
Government subpoena	73.6
Intellectual property	73.9
Fraud or false claims	75.2
Employment	79.5
Intellectual property	81.1
Intellectual property	81.4
Government subpoena	81.5
Intellectual property	82.1
Government subpoena	84.2
Contract	85.6
Product liability	86.8
Product liability	87.6
Product liability	88.8
Antitrust	88.8
Intellectual property	88.9
Government subpoena	90.7
Product liability	91.8
Fraud or false claims	91.8
Contract	93.8

Table A.7
Internal Expenditures as a Percentage of All Production Costs, $13,000 Added to All Reported Internal Expenditures, 41 Cases

Subject Matter	Internal Expenditures as a Percentage of Total Costs
Product liability	0.0
Product liability	0.1
Antitrust	0.2
Employment	0.2
Product liability	0.3
Government subpoena	0.4
Fraud or false claims	0.4
Government subpoena	0.4
Fraud or false claims	0.5
Intellectual property	0.5
Product liability	0.6
Antitrust	0.6
Intellectual property	0.6
Product liability	0.6
Intellectual property	0.7
Government subpoena	0.7
Contract	1.0
Intellectual property	1.2
Intellectual property	2.2
Fraud or false claims	3.2
Contract	4.1
Intellectual property	4.5
Contract	4.6
Fraud or false claims	4.9
Government subpoena	6.5
Government subpoena	6.5
Intellectual property	7.1
Product liability	7.5
Intellectual property	7.5
Government subpoena	8.0
Intellectual property	8.6

Table A.7—Continued

Subject Matter	Internal Expenditures as a Percentage of Total Costs
Contract	9.4
Government subpoena	9.9
Intellectual property	10.5
Intellectual property	13.6
Intellectual property	14.5
Government subpoena	20.4
Product liability	25.1
Government subpoena	36.3
Intellectual property	43.1
Insurance	43.8

Table A.8
Vendor Expenditures as a Percentage of All Production Costs, $13,000 Added to All Reported Internal Expenditures, 41 Cases

Subject Matter	Vendor Expenditures as a Percentage of Total Costs
Product liability	0.0
Product liability	4.4
Contract	6.1
Intellectual property	7.7
Fraud or false claims	8.2
Product liability	8.2
Intellectual property	8.9
Contract	10.1
Intellectual property	11.0
Antitrust	11.2
Product liability	11.2
Product liability	12.4
Intellectual property	15.5
Intellectual property	15.5
Government subpoena	15.7
Government subpoena	16.7
Government subpoena	18.4
Intellectual property	18.5

Table A.8—Continued

Subject Matter	Vendor Expenditures as a Percentage of Total Costs
Employment	20.4
Fraud or false claims	22.3
Government subpoena	26.2
Fraud or false claims	27.4
Antitrust	27.8
Product liability	28.0
Intellectual property	28.1
Intellectual property	28.2
Intellectual property	28.4
Fraud or false claims	30.3
Intellectual property	30.3
Insurance	31.2
Contract	34.0
Government subpoena	34.1
Product liability	39.5
Government subpoena	41.6
Intellectual property	41.9
Intellectual property	43.2
Government subpoena	51.7
Government subpoena	63.7
Intellectual property	73.5
Contract	90.6
Government subpoena	93.5

Table A.9
Outside Counsel Expenditures as a Percentage of All Production Costs, $13,000 Added to All Reported Internal Expenditures, 41 Cases

Subject Matter	Outside Counsel Expenditures as a Percentage of Total Costs
Contractual	0.0
Government subpoena	0.0
Government subpoena	0.0
Insurance	25.0
Intellectual property	25.3

Table A.9—Continued

Subject Matter	Outside Counsel Expenditures as a Percentage of Total Costs
Product liability	35.4
Government subpoena	41.8
Intellectual property	46.3
Intellectual property	49.2
Government subpoena	50.4
Government subpoena	53.4
Intellectual property	57.4
Intellectual property	57.5
Contract	61.9
Intellectual property	63.2
Fraud or false claims	64.8
Government subpoena	65.6
Intellectual property	67.1
Intellectual property	67.4
Intellectual property	70.9
Antitrust	71.6
Product liability	71.9
Fraud or false claims	72.2
Government subpoena	73.4
Fraud or false claims	74.5
Intellectual property	77.4
Employment	79.4
Intellectual property	80.9
Government subpoena	80.9
Intellectual property	83.6
Government subpoena	83.9
Contract	85.3
Product liability	87.1
Intellectual property	88.5
Product liability	88.5
Antitrust	88.7
Fraud or false claims	91.3
Product liability	91.7

Table A.9—Continued

Subject Matter	Outside Counsel Expenditures as a Percentage of Total Costs
Product liability	92.5
Contract	92.8
Product liability	95.0

APPENDIX B

Recall, Precision, and Other Performance Measures

Two important concepts to understand when assessing the effectiveness of computer-categorized review techniques, such as predictive coding, are *recall* and *precision*. In information-retrieval science, *recall* is a measurement of completeness, essentially describing how well a process identifies items of specific interest compared with the total number of such items that exist in a set of data or documents. *Precision* is a measurement of efficiency, describing how well a process identifies only those items of specific interest, by comparing the number of target items identified with the total number of documents retrieved. Alternative terms for *recall* and *precision* sometimes found in information-retrieval literature are *sensitivity* and *positive predictive value* (PPV), respectively.

Assume, for example, that, in a set of 1,000 documents, exactly 200 discuss fruits while the other 800 discuss only crayon colors. A person is tasked with the job of searching through the documents to find all of those discussing fruit. A search that looked only for the terms "mulberry," "kiwifruit," and "orange" yielded 90 documents. However, only 60 were truly successful matches (*true positives*) because the word "orange" was also found in 30 documents about crayon colors, resulting in the erroneous identification of those documents as fruit-related (*false positives*). Table B.1 presents the results of the search. Of the 910 documents that the search essentially determined to have nothing to do with fruits (because the terms used did not identify them as being of interest), 140 were actually fruit-related (and can therefore be thought of as *false negatives*) while the remaining 770 documents were accurate assessments of a lack of any discussion of fruits (*true negatives*).

The recall rate can be calculated by dividing the number of true positives returned by the search (60) by the total number of fruit-related documents in the entire set (200), for a rate of 30 percent. The precision rate can be calculated by dividing the number of true positives

Table B.1
Example Showing Recall and Precision: Results of Search for Fruit-Related Documents

	Actual Numbers in Set	
Search Result	**Documents Discussing Fruit (n = 200)**	**Documents Not Discussing Fruit (n = 800)**
Indicated fruit discussion (n = 90)	60 (true positives)	30 (false positives)
Indicated no fruit discussion (n = 910)	140 (false negatives)	770 (true negatives)

returned by the search (60) by the number of documents the search indicated as fruit related (90), for a rate of 67 percent.

Ideally, both recall and precision rates will approach 100 percent. However, in the information-retrieval context, precision and recall rates are often inversely related. When the searcher added the terms "pomegranate," "lychee," and "lemon" to the original three terms and then performed the search again, 600 documents were flagged, with 150 of those flagged documents actually exhibiting the desired relationship with fruit ("orange" and "lemon" were also present in 450 documents concerning crayons). Expanding the search terms thus resulted in a better recall rate (75 percent, 150 divided by 200) but a lower precision rate (25 percent, 150 divided by 600).

One way to view these measures is that lower recall rates increase the risk that the search will miss what is important, while lower precision rates indicate less efficient results. In the context of a document review intended to reduce the production set to only those documents that are both relevant and responsive, a process that reflects a low recall rate will result in a failure to provide the demanding party with a substantial portion of the information to which it is legally entitled. The ramifications of such a failure can include sanctions and other undesirable outcomes. Should the process reflect a low precision rate, the document set delivered to the demanding party will contain an abundance of irrelevant or nonresponsive documents, perhaps leading to claims of overproduction for the purpose of hiding important evidence and a judicial order to redo the review (there may also be additional costs to the producing party to process such an unnecessarily large volume of documents).

To describe this relationship between recall and precision, a statistic known as the *F-measure* calculates the harmonic mean of precision and recall, defined as

$$2\left(\frac{\text{precision} \times \text{recall}}{\text{precision} + \text{recall}}\right).$$

Larger F-measures indicate better overall results as measured by the balance between recall and precision. According to the F-measure, the first search that just used three terms was actually the more effective one when both recall and precision are taken into account, compared with the second, which used six terms (0.414 versus 0.375).

Because of the tendency for recall and precision to be inversely related, litigants (and judges deciding discovery issues) may be placed in a position requiring a choice as to whether it is more important to maximize the likelihood that all documents of interest will be found or minimize the percentage of documents yielded by the search that are false positives. The demanding party, for example, might be amenable to a process that results in a modest recall rate if doing so increases the precision rate to a point at which the production is of relatively manageable volume and therefore less costly to analyze. On the other hand, if it were vitally important to identify as many items of potential interest as possible regardless of cost (such as might be required during a criminal investigation), then a higher recall rate would be sought. Thus, it is not true that highest F-measures are always the most desirable.

Two other measures commonly used in the literature are *specificity* and *negative predictive value* (NPV). They can be viewed as complementary to the concepts of recall and precision (or sensitivity and PPV, to use the alternative terminology) but with a focus on true negatives rather than true positives. Although recall is a way to describe how well the process identifies items of interest, specificity is calculated by dividing the number of true negatives by the total number of items that do *not* meet the specified criteria. In the example above, there were actually 800 documents that had nothing to do with fruits, while the initial search correctly reported that 770 documents were non–fruit-related. Thus, specificity would be 96.25 percent (770 divided by 800).[1] In a similar way, NPV complements precision by dividing the number of true negatives (77) by the total number of items the search indicated as not fruit-related (910). Thus, NPV in this example would be 77.8 percent.

---

[1] A commonly employed example of the relationship between specificity and recall (or sensitivity) involves the threshold settings for airport metal detectors and other security scanners. Reducing the setting at which an alarm would be triggered would lower the rate of specificity because additional passengers would be subjected to a search even if they carry nothing more than a small amount of coins or jewelry. In other words, the proportion of true negatives (passengers who pose no threat) who are approved by the scanners would be reduced. On the other hand, the lower settings would pick up a greater proportion of passengers carrying metal objects that could potentially be used as weapons, thus yielding a higher rate of recall.

References

ABA—*See* American Bar Association.

Akers, Steve, Jennifer Keadle Mason, and Peter L. Mansmann, "An Intelligent Approach to E-Discovery," *DESI IV: The ICAIL 2011 Workshop on Setting Standards for Searching Electronically Stored Information in Discovery Proceedings*, c. 2011. As of September 20, 2011:
http://www.umiacs.umd.edu/~oard/desi4/papers/akers.pdf

Allman, Thomas Y., "Preservation Rulemaking After the 2010 Litigation Conference," *Sedona Conference Journal*, Vol. 11, Fall 2010, pp. 217–228.

———, *State E-Discovery Today: An Assessment and Update of Rulemaking*, February 23, 2011a. As of June 30, 2011:
http://works.bepress.com/context/thomas_allman/article/1000/type/native/viewcontent

———, "Rules Committee Memo," *The Electronic Discovery Counselor*, April 20, 2011b. As of May 11, 2011:
http://www.fiosinc.com/publications/newsletter_article.aspx?id=784

Allman, Thomas Y., Jason R. Baron, and Maura R. Grossman, *Preservation, Search Technology and Rulemaking*, submission to the Discovery Subcommittee of the Advisory Committee on Civil Rules, Committee on Rules of Practice and Procedure of the Judicial Conference of the United States regarding the September 9, 2011, Mini-Conference on Preservation and Sanctions, September 7, 2011.

Altman Weil, "Law Department Managers Hold the Line on Spending," *Metropolitan Corporate Counsel*, October 1, 2004. As of February 22, 2012:
http://www.metrocorpcounsel.com/articles/4649/law-department-managers-hold-line-spending

American Bar Association, *Report of Pound Conference Follow-Up Task Force*, Chicago, Ill., August 1976.

———, Section of Litigation, *Second Report of the Special Committee for the Study of Discovery Abuse*, Chicago, Ill., November 1980.

———, Commission on the Impact of the Economic Crises on the Profession and Legal Needs, *The Value Proposition of Attending Law School*, Chicago, Ill., November 2009a. As of July 5, 2011:
http://www.americanbar.org/content/dam/aba/migrated/lsd/legaled/value.authcheckdam.pdf

———, Section of Litigation, *ABA Section of Litigation Member Survey on Civil Practice: Full Report*, December 11, 2009b. As of February 22, 2012:
http://www.americanbar.org/content/dam/aba/migrated/litigation/survey/docs/report_aba_report.authcheckdam.pdf

Anseel, Frederik, Filip Lievens, Eveline Schollaert, and Beata Choragwicka, "Response Rates in Organizational Science, 1995–2008: A Meta-Analytic Review and Guidelines for Survey Researchers," *Journal of Business and Psychology*, Vol. 25, No. 3, September 2010, pp. 335–349.

Association of Corporate Counsel, "In-House Counsel Increasingly Hold Outside Counsel More Accountable, Using Metrics and Technology to Track Results," press release, October 29, 2007. As of January 6, 2011:
http://www.acc.com/aboutacc/newsroom/pressreleases/2005/OUTSIDE-COUNSEL-MORE-ACCOUNTABLE.cfm

Attenex, "Proven to Save Time and Expense by Up to 75%," undated. As of August 26, 2011:
http://198.173.75.214/products/eDiscovery/timeExpense/

Austin, Doug, "eDiscovery Best Practices: Does Size Matter?" *eDiscovery Daily*, March 25, 2011. As of September 8, 2011:
http://www.ediscoverydaily.com/2011/03/ediscovery-best-practices-does-size-matter.html

Barlyn, Suzanne, "Call My Lawyer . . . in India," *Time*, April 3, 2008. As of February 22, 2012:
http://www.time.com/time/magazine/article/0,9171,1727726,00.html

Barnett, Thomas I., and Svetlana Godjevac, "Faster, Better, Cheaper Legal Document Review, Pipe Dream or Reality?" *ICAIL 2011/DESI IV: Workshop on Setting Standards for Searching Electronically Stored Information in Discovery Proceedings*, June 6, 2011. As of September 20, 2011:
http://www.umiacs.umd.edu/~oard/desi4/proceedings.pdf

Barnett, Thomas, Svetlana Godjevac, Jean-Michel Renders, Caroline Privault, John Schneider, and Robert Wickstrom, *Machine Learning Classification for Document Review*, paper presented at Workshop DESI at the 12th International Conference on Artificial Intelligence and Law (ICAIL 2009), June 8, 2009. As of June 2, 2011:
http://www.law.pitt.edu/DESI3_Workshop/Papers/DESI_III.Xerox_Barnett.Xerox.pdf

Baron, Jason R., "Law in the Age of Exabytes: Some Further Thoughts on 'Information Inflation' and Current Issues in E-Discovery Search," *Richmond Journal of Law and Technology*, Vol. 17, Issue 3, Art. 9, Spring 2011. As of February 22, 2012:
http://jolt.richmond.edu/v17i3/article9.pdf

Beisner, John H., *The Centre Cannot Hold: The Need for Effective Reform of the U.S. Civil Discovery Process*, Washington, D.C.: U.S. Chamber Institute for Legal Reform, May 2010. As of February 22, 2012:
http://www.uschamber.com/reports/centre-cannot-hold-need-effective-reform-us-civil-discovery-process

Bennitt, Jane, "With First Phase Complete, LEDES Oversight Committee Seeks Feedback," *Law Technology News*, March 11, 2011.

BLS—*See* Bureau of Labor Statistics.

Borden, Bennett B., "The Demise of Linear Review," *E-Discovery Alert,* October 2010. As of February 22, 2012:
http://www.williamsmullen.com/the-demise-of-linear-review-10-01-2010/

Borden, Bennett B., Monica McCarroll, Mark Cordover, and Sam Strickland, *Why Document Review Is Broken*, Williams Mullen, May 16, 2011. As of October 3, 2011:
http://www.williamsmullen.com/resources/detail.aspx?pub=664

Brazil, Wayne D., "Civil Discovery: Lawyer's Views of Its Effectiveness, Its Principal Problems and Abuses," *American Bar Foundation Research Journal*, Vol. 5, No. 4, Autumn 1980, pp. 787–902.

Brown, Gillian, and George Yule, *Discourse Analysis*, Cambridge, UK: Cambridge University Press, 1983.

Bureau of Labor Statistics, "Table 5. Employer Costs per Hour Worked for Employee Compensation and Costs as a Percent of Total Compensation: Private Industry Workers, by Major Occupational Group and Bargaining Unit Status, March 2011," *Economic News Release*, March 2011a.

———, "May 2010 National Industry-Specific Occupational Employment and Wage Estimates: NAICS 551100—Management of Companies and Enterprises," *Occupational Employment Statistics*, last modified May 16, 2011b. As of July 6, 2011:
http://www.bls.gov/oes/current/naics4_551100.htm

Campbell, James M., "The Need for Discovery Reform," *Defense Counsel Journal*, Vol. 77, No. 1, January 2010, p. 3.

Carlson, Scott A., "New EDD Tools Promise Better Performance," *New Jersey Law Journal*, March 22, 2006.

Childress, Robert, "How to Handle Duplicate and Near-Duplicate Documents Throughout Discovery and Review," *Lextek: Chicago Lawyer's Tek Talk*, 2009. As of May 11, 2011:
http://lextekreport.com/2009/05/20/
how-to-handle-duplicate-and-near-duplicate-documents-throughout-discovery-and-review/

Clay, Thomas S., and Eric A. Seeger, *2010 Law Firms in Transition: An Altman Weil Flash Survey*, Newtown Square, Pa.: Altman Weil, June 22, 2010. As of February 22, 2012:
http://www.altmanweil.com/LFiT2010/

Clearwell Systems, "Customer Case Study: Saint Barnabas Health Care System," 2010. As of July 8, 2011:
http://www.cetratechnology.com/documents/CW_CS_Saint_Barnabus.pdf

Cohen, William W., "Enron Email Dataset," last modified August 21, 2009. As of February 24, 2012:
http://www.cs.cmu.edu/~enron/

Compliance, Governance and Oversight Council and Huron Consulting Group, *Benchmark Survey on Prevailing Practices for Legal Holds in Global 1000 Companies*, 2008. As of July 6, 2011:
http://www.huronconsultinggroup.com/library/CGOC_Huron_Benchmarks_Final.pdf

Connolly, Paul R., Edith A. Holleman, and Michael J. Kuhlman, *Judicial Controls and the Civil Litigative Process: Discovery*, Washington, D.C.: Federal Judicial Center, 1978.

Cormack, Gordon V., and Mona Mojdeh, "Machine Learning for Information Retrieval: TREC 2009 Web, Relevance Feedback and Legal Tracks," *The Eighteenth Text REtrieval Conference (TREC 2009) Proceedings*, 2010. As of April 3, 2011:
http://trec.nist.gov/pubs/trec18/papers/uwaterloo-cormack.WEB.RF.LEGAL.pdf

Cotts, Cynthia, and Liane Kufchock, "U.S. Firms Outsource Legal Services to India," *New York Times*, August 21, 2007. As of February 22, 2012:
http://www.nytimes.com/2007/08/21/business/worldbusiness/21iht-law.4.7199252.html

Degnan, David, "Accounting for the Costs of Electronic Discovery," *Minnesota Journal of Law, Science and Technology*, Vol. 12, No. 1, 2011, pp. 151–190.

Dertouzos, James N., Nicholas M. Pace, and Robert H. Anderson, *The Legal and Economic Implications of Electronic Discovery: Options for Future Research*, Santa Monica, Calif.: RAND Corporation, OP-183-ICJ, 2008. As of February 22, 2012:
http://www.rand.org/pubs/occasional_papers/OP183.html

Deutchman, Leonard, "Getting Ready for the Rules Changes, Part VIII," *Pennsylvania Law Weekly*, May 21, 2007.

Doherty, Sean, "Judge Peck Addresses Predictive Coding in Federal Court Order," *Law Technology News*, February 14, 2012.

"Down in the Data Mines," *ABA Journal*, December 1, 2008. As of February 22, 2012:
http://www.abajournal.com/magazine/article/down_in_the_data_mines/

Drahozal, Christopher R., and Laura J. Hines, "Secrecy and Transparency in Dispute Resolution: Secret Settlement Restrictions and Unintended Consequences," *Kansas Law Review*, Vol. 54, 2006, pp. 1457–1484.

Driver, Albert W., "Near-Duplicates: The Elephant in the Document Review Room," *Metropolitan Corporate Counsel*, Vol. 15, No. 1, January 1, 2007. As of February 22, 2012:
http://www.metrocorpcounsel.com/articles/7757/near-duplicates-elephant-document-review-room

———, "Do Your Bit to Control Runaway E-Discovery Costs," *Metropolitan Corporate Counsel*, Vol. 18, No. 4, April 5, 2010a. As of February 22, 2012:
http://www.metrocorpcounsel.com/articles/12501/do-your-bit-control-runaway-e-discovery-costs

———, "Fight Runaway E-Discovery Costs: How You Can Help," *Metropolitan Corporate Counsel*, Vol. 18, No. 4, April 5, 2010b. As of February 22, 2012:
http://www.metrocorpcounsel.com/articles/12428/fight-runaway-e-discovery-costs-how-you-can-help

———, "Predictive Coding = Great E-Discovery Cost and Time Savings," *Metropolitan Corporate Counsel*, Vol. 19, No. 12, November 16, 2011. As of February 22, 2012:
http://www.epiqsystems.com/uploadedFiles/Epiq_in_the_News/MCC_Baker_Laing.pdf

Dutton, Cliff, "eOPS 2010: Electronic Discovery Operational Parameters Survey—Executive Summary," April 2010. As of August 20, 2011:
http://www.catalystsecure.com/blog/wp-content/uploads/2011/07/
Electronic-Discovery-Operational-Parameters-Survey.pdf

Economic Analysis Group, "Internal Timekeeping," undated. As of May 7, 2011:
http://www.case-track.com/inttimekeeping.html

EDRM—*See* Electronic Discovery Reference Model.

Efthimiadis, Efthimis N., and Mary A. Hotchkiss, "Legal Discovery: Does Domain Expertise Matter?" *Proceedings of the American Society for Information Science and Technology*, Vol. 45, Issue 1, 2008, pp. 1–2.

Egan, Chris, and Glen Homer, "Achieve Savings by Predicting and Controlling Total Discovery Cost," *Metropolitan Corporate Counsel*, Vol. 16, No. 12, December 1, 2008, p. 8. As of February 22, 2012:
http://www.metrocorpcounsel.com/articles/10725/
achieve-savings-predicting-and-controlling-total-discovery-cost

Electronic Discovery Reference Model, "Collection Guide," undated (a). As of February 24, 2012:
http://www.edrm.net/resources/guides/edrm-framework-guides/collection

———, "EDRM Metrics Code Set," undated (b). As of July 17, 2011:
http://www.edrm.net/resources/standards/edrm-metrics/edrm-metrics-code-set

———, "EDRM Stages," undated (c). As of February 24, 2012:
http://www.edrm.net/resources/edrm-stages-explained

———, "Frequently Asked Questions," undated (d). As of May 7, 2011:
http://www.edrm.net/joining-edrm/frequently-asked-questions

———, "Information Governance Reference Model (IGRM)," undated (e). As of February 24, 2012:
http://www.edrm.net/projects/igrm

———, "Presentation Guide," undated (f). As of February 24, 2012:
http://www.edrm.net/resources/guides/edrm-framework-guides/presentation-guid

———, "Preservation Guide," undated (g). As of February 24, 2012:
http://www.edrm.net/resources/guides/edrm-framework-guides/preservation

———, "Processing Guide," undated (h). As of February 24, 2012:
http://www.edrm.net/resources/guides/edrm-framework-guides/processing

———, "Identification Guide," updated November 3, 2010a. As of February 24, 2012:
http://www.edrm.net/resources/guides/edrm-framework-guides/identification

———, "Production Guide," updated November 4, 2010b. As of February 24, 2012:
http://www.edrm.net/resources/guides/edrm-framework-guides/production

———, "Analysis Guide," updated November 30, 2010c. As of February 24, 2012:
http://www.edrm.net/resources/guides/edrm-framework-guides/analysis

———, "Review Guide," updated December 9, 2010d. As of February 24, 2012:
http://www.edrm.net/resources/guides/edrm-framework-guides/review-guide

Epiq Systems, "ACC Quick Hit Presentation: Document Review Efficiency," January 13, 2009. As of August 20, 2011:
http://author.acc.com/committees/ldmc/upload/ACC-Quick-Hit-Supplement-Epiq.pdf

Equivio, *Proposed Guidelines for Measuring the Benefit of Technology for Managing Redundant Data in E-Discovery Review*, undated. As of March 9, 2012:
http://www.equivio.com/files/files/White%20Paper%20-%20Proposed%20Guidelines%20for%20
Measuring%20the%20Benefit%20of%20Technology%20for%20Managing%20Redundant%20Data%20
in%20E-Discovery%20Review.pdf

———, *Am Law 100 Firm Uses Equivio>Relevance™ to Find More Relevant Documents and to Find Them Faster: an Epiq-Equivio Case Study*, 2009a.

———, *Near-Duplicate Detection in Electronic and OCR Collections*, 2009b.

Fleiss, Joseph L., Bruce A. Levin, and Myunghee Cho Paik, *Statistical Methods for Rates and Proportions*, 3rd ed., Hoboken, N.J.: J. Wiley, 2003.

Fulbright and Jaworski, *Fulbright's 6th Annual Litigation Trends Survey Report*, 2009. As of January 3, 2011: http://amlawdaily.typepad.com/fulbrightreport2009.pdf

Glaser, William A., *Pretrial Discovery and the Adversary System*, New York: Russell Sage Foundation, 1968.

Greenwood, Arin, "Attorney at Blah," *Washington City Paper*, November 8, 2007. As of July 5, 2011: http://www.washingtoncitypaper.com/articles/34054/attorney-at-blah

Grimm, Paul W., Lisa Yurmit Bergstrom, and Matthew P. Kraeuter, "Federal Rule of Evidence 502: Has It Lived Up to Its Potential?" *Richmond Journal of Law and Technology*, Vol. 17, No. 3, Art. 8, Spring 2011.

Groom, Tom, *Predictive Coding: Gain Earlier Insight and Reduce Document Review Costs*, Discovery Engineering, May 2011. As of September 3, 2011: http://www.coalsm.org/files/D4_-_Predictive_Coding_Seminar.pdf

Grossman, Maura R., and Gordon V. Cormack, "Technology-Assisted Review in E-Discovery Can Be More Effective and More Efficient Than Exhaustive Manual Review," *Richmond Journal of Law and Technology*, Vol. 17, No. 3, Art. 11, Spring 2011a. As of February 22, 2012: http://jolt.richmond.edu/v17i3/article11.pdf

———, "Inconsistent Assessment of Responsiveness in E-Discovery: Difference of Opinion or Human Error?" *DESI IV: The ICAIL 2011 Workshop on Setting Standards for Searching Electronically Stored Information in Discovery Proceedings*, June 6, 2011b. As of September 3, 2011: http://www.umiacs.umd.edu/~oard/desi4/papers/grossman3.pdf

Hall, Rich, and Brian Johnson, "Legal Enterprise Management: A New Level of Control for Corporate Legal Departments," *Case/Matter Management*, International Legal Technology Association, July 2010, pp. 34–38.

Hamburg, Rebecca M., Matthew C. Koski, and Paul H. Tobias, *Summary of Results of Federal Judicial Center Survey of NELA Members, Fall 2009*, March 26, 2010. As of February 22, 2012: http://www.uscourts.gov/uscourts/RulesAndPolicies/rules/Duke%20Materials/Library/NELA,%20Summary%20of%20Results%20of%20FJC%20Survey%20of%20NELA%20Members.pdf

Harrington, Michael J., deputy general counsel, Eli Lilly and Company; Theodore B. Van Itallie Jr., associate general counsel, Johnson and Johnson; James K. Grasty, vice president and general counsel, Merck and Company; Charna L. Gerstenhaber, executive director and head of litigation, Novartis Pharmaceuticals Corporation; David Reid, senior vice president and managing director of the legal division, Pfizer; and William J. Ruane, vice president and associate general counsel for litigation, Wyeth; letter to Russell G. Golden, technical director, Financial Accounting Standards Board, August 8, 2008. As of February 3, 2011: http://www.pharmalot.com/wp-content/uploads/2008/08/fasb-letter.pdf

HaystackID, "Data Processing," 2011.

Hedin, Bruce, Stephen Tomlinson, Jason R. Baron, and Douglas W. Oard, "Overview of the TREC 2009 Legal Track," *The Eighteenth Text REtrieval Conference (TREC 2009) Proceedings*, 2010. As of May 18, 2011: http://trec.nist.gov/pubs/trec18/papers/LEGAL09.OVERVIEW.pdf

Heilman, Lori, "Federal Courts' Reactions to Inadequate Keyword Searches: Moving Toward a Predictable and Consistent Standard for Attorneys Employing Keyword Searches," *University of Cincinnati Law Review*, Vol. 78, 2010, pp. 1103–1127.

helpme123, *Temporary Attorney: The Sweatshop Edition*, undated blog.

———, "Juristaff," *Temporary Attorney: The Sweatshop Edition*, October 19, 2009, 3:40 p.m. As of June 22, 2011:
http://temporaryattorney.blogspot.com/2009/10/juristaff.html

Hensler, Deborah R., *Why We Don't Know More About the Civil Justice System, and What We Could Do About It*, Santa Monica, Calif.: RAND Corporation, RP-363, 1995. As of February 22, 2012: http://www.rand.org/pubs/reprints/RP363.html

Hogan, Christopher, Dan Brassil, Shana M. Rugani, Jennifer Reinhart, Misti Gerber, and Teresa Jade, "H5 at TREC 2008 Legal Interactive: User Modeling, Assessment and Measurement," *Proceedings of the 17th Text Retrieval Conference (TREC 2008)*, 2009. As of July 6, 2011: http://trec.nist.gov/pubs/trec17/papers/h5.legal.rev.pdf

"How, and How Much, Do Lawyers Charge?" *Lawyers.com*, undated. As of August 20, 2011:
http://research.lawyers.com/How-and-How-Much-Do-Lawyers-Charge.html

Howard, David M., Jonathan Palmer, and Joe Banks, Microsoft Corporation, *Letter to the Honorable David G. Campbell*, submission to the Discovery Subcommittee of the Advisory Committee on Civil Rules, Committee on Rules of Practice and Procedure of the Judicial Conference of the United States regarding the September 9, 2011, Mini-Conference on Preservation and Sanctions, August 31, 2011.

Hubbard, William H. J., *Preliminary Report on the Preservation Costs Survey of Major Companies*, submission to the Discovery Subcommittee of the Advisory Committee on Civil Rules, Committee on Rules of Practice and Procedure of the Judicial Conference of the United States regarding the September 9, 2011, Mini-Conference on Preservation and Sanctions, September 8, 2011.

IBM, *Mining Mountains of Evidence*, December 16, 2010. As of September 17, 2011:
http://www-01.ibm.com/software/success/cssdb.nsf/CS/KKMH-8BBQ2M?OpenDocument&Site=default&cty=en_us

Institute for the Advancement of the American Legal System, *Interim Report and 2008 Litigation Survey of the Fellows of the American College of Trial Lawyers on the Joint Project of the American College of Trial Lawyers Task Force on Discovery and the Institute for the Advancement of the American Legal System*, September 9, 2008. As of March 9, 2012:
http://iaals.du.edu/images/wygwam/documents/publications/Interim_Report_Final_for_web.pdf

Intelligent Discovery Management, "Efficiently Reduce Document Sets in a Defensible Manner," undated. As of September 26, 2011:
http://www.idmlitsup.com/processing-and-analysis/near-duplicate-detection.php

IPRO Tech, "IPRO SaaS," undated. As of September 17, 2011:
http://www.iprotech.com/saas/

Iris Data Services, "Unify," 2009. As of September 17, 2011:
http://www.irisds.com/files/brochures/onlinereview-Unify.pdf

JAMS, "JAMS Recommended Arbitration Discovery Protocols for Domestic, Commercial Cases," effective January 6, 2010. As of January 3, 2011:
http://www.jamsadr.com/files/Uploads/Documents/JAMS-Rules/JAMS_Arbitration_Discovery_Protocols.pdf

Judicial Conference of the United States, Committee on Rules of Practice and Procedure, *Revised Preliminary Draft of Proposed Amendments to the Federal Rules of Civil Procedure*, Washington, D.C., February 1979.

———, Advisory Committee on Civil Rules, "2010 Civil Litigation Conference," c. 2010a, referenced January 6, 2011. As of February 22, 2012:
http://www.uscourts.gov/RulesAndPolicies/FederalRulemaking/Overview/DukeWebsiteMsg.aspx

———, Advisory Committee on Civil Rules and the Committee on Rules of Practice and Procedure, *Report to the Chief Justice of the United States on the 2010 Conference on Civil Litigation*, c. 2010b. As of February 22, 2012:
http://www.uscourts.gov/uscourts/RulesAndPolicies/rules/2010%20report.pdf

Kakalik, James S., Terence Dunworth, Laural A. Hill, Daniel F. McCaffrey, Marian Oshiro, Nicholas M. Pace, and Mary E. Vaiana, *An Evaluation of Judicial Case Management Under the Civil Justice Reform Act*, Santa Monica, Calif.: RAND Corporation, MR-802-ICJ, 1996. As of February 22, 2012:
http://www.rand.org/pubs/monograph_reports/MR802.html

Kakalik, James S., Deborah R. Hensler, Daniel F. McCaffrey, Marian Oshiro, Nicholas M. Pace, and Mary E. Vaiana, *Discovery Management: Further Analysis of the Civil Justice Reform Act Evaluation Data*, Santa Monica, Calif.: RAND Corporation, MR-941-ICJ, 1998. As of February 22, 2012:
http://www.rand.org/pubs/monograph_reports/MR941.html

KCura, "Go Faster," undated. As of September 27, 2011:
http://kcura.com/relativity/advantages/go-faster

Kershaw, Anne, "Automated Document Review Proves Its Reliability," *Digital Discovery and e-Evidence*, Vol. 5, No. 11, November 2005, pp. 10–12. As of February 22, 2012:
http://www.h5.com/pdf/autodocreview.pdf

Kershaw, Anne, and Joseph Howie, *Report on Kershaw-Howie Survey of E-Discovery Providers Pertaining to Email Threading*, Tarrytown, N.Y.: Electronic Discovery Institute, January 5, 2010a. As of February 22, 2012: http://www.electronicdiscoveryinstitute.com/pubs/eDiscoveryInstituteThreadingReportFinal_JH.pdf

———, *eDiscovery Institute Survey on Predictive Coding*, Tarrytown, N.Y.: eDiscovery Institute, October 1, 2010b. As of February 22, 2012: http://www.ediscoveryinstitute.org/publications/ediscovery_institute_survey_on_predictive_coding

Kessler, Daniel P., and Daniel L. Rubinfeld, "Empirical Study of the Civil Justice System," in A. Mitchell Polinsky and Steven Shavell, eds., *Handbook of Law and Economics*, Vol. 1, North Holland, Netherlands: Elsevier, 2007, pp. 345–402.

Klimt, Bryan, and Yiming Yang, "The Enron Corpus: A New Dataset for Email Classification Research," in Jean-François Boulicaut, Floriana Esposito, Fosca Giannotti, and Dino Pedreschi, eds., *Machine Learning: ECML 2004, 15th European Conference on Machine Learning, Pisa, Italy, September 20–24, 2004, Proceedings*, 2004, pp. 217–226.

Koblentz, Evan, "Bragging Rights or Blowing Smoke?" *Law Technology News*, August 1, 2011.

Kolker, Carlyn, "SEC Cracks Down on Disclosure of Lawsuit Costs," *Thomson Reuters News and Insight*, February 3, 2011. As of June 22, 2011: http://newsandinsight.thomsonreuters.com/Legal/news/2011/02_-_february/sec_cracks_down_on_disclosure_of_lawsuit_costs/

Krause, Jason, "TREC 2008 Stresses Human Element in EDD," *Law Technology News*, May 1, 2009.

———, "Businesses Head Off E-Discovery Costs," *Law Technology News*, February 25, 2011.

Kritzer, Herbert M., "The Civil Litigation Research Project: Lessons for Studying the Civil Justice System," in Alan E. Gelfand, ed., *Proceedings of the Second Workshop on Law and Justice Statistics*, Washington, D.C.: U.S. Department of Justice, Bureau of Justice Statistics, 1983, pp. 30–36.

Kubacki, Kelly, Michele Lange, and David Meadows, Kroll Ontrack, *Letter to the Honorable David G. Campbell*, submission to the Discovery Subcommittee of the Advisory Committee on Civil Rules, Committee on Rules of Practice and Procedure of the Judicial Conference of the United States regarding the September 9, 2011, Mini-Conference on Preservation and Sanctions, August 31, 2011.

Lacey, Dominic, Jamie Tanner, and James Moeskops, "Case Study: Predicting the Future of Disclosure," *Smart E-Discovery*, undated. As of February 20, 2012: http://blog.millnet.co.uk/index.php/tools-and-technologies/case-study-predicting-the-future-of-disclosure/

Landauer, Thomas K., and Susan T. Dumais, "A Solution to Plato's Problem: The Latent Semantic Analysis Theory of Acquisition, Induction, and Representation of Knowledge," *Psychological Review*, Vol. 104, No. 2, 1997, pp. 211–240.

Lange, Michele C. S., and Kristin M. Nimsger, *Electronic Evidence and Discovery: What Every Lawyer Should Know Now*, 2nd ed., Chicago, Ill.: ABA Publishing, 2009.

Lawyers for Civil Justice, *Comment to the Civil Rules Advisory Committee: A Prescription for Stronger Medicine—Narrow the Scope of Discovery*, September 1, 2010. As of March 9, 2012: http://lfcj.digidoq.com/BLAP/Lawyers%20for%20Civil%20Justice/FRCP%20Discovery%20Comment%20FINAL%20090110.pdf

Lawyers for Civil Justice, Civil Justice Reform Group, and U.S. Chamber Institute for Legal Reform, *Litigation Cost Survey of Major Companies*, May 2010. As of March 9, 2012: http://www.uscourts.gov/uscourts/RulesAndPolicies/rules/Duke%20Materials/Library/Litigation%20Cost%20Survey%20of%20Major%20Companies.pdf

Lawyers for Civil Justice, DRI, Federation of Defense and Corporate Counsel, and International Association of Defense Counsel, *Reshaping the Rules of Civil Procedure for the 21st Century: The Need for Clear, Concise, and Meaningful Amendments to Key Rules of Civil Procedure*, May 2, 2010. As of May 3, 2011: http://www.dri.org/ContentDirectory/Public/CommitteeDocs/0440/Reshaping%20the%20Rules%20of%20Civil%20Procedure%20for%20the%2021st%20Century.pdf

Lee, Emery G. III, and Thomas E. Willging, *Federal Judicial Center National, Case-Based Civil Rules Survey: Preliminary Report to the Judicial Conference Advisory Committee on Civil Rules*, Washington, D.C.: Federal Judicial Center, October 2009.

———, "Defining the Problem of Cost in Federal Civil Litigation," *Duke Law Journal*, Vol. 60, December 2010, pp. 765–788.

Legal Electronic Data Exchange Standard Oversight Committee, "Uniform Task Based Management System (UTBMS)," undated. As of July 3, 2011:
http://utbms.com/

Lewis, David D., "Interassessor Consistency Data on TREC 06 Legal Track Ad Hoc Topics," ireval@nist.gov, January 31, 2007. As of June 15, 2011:
http://cio.nist.gov/esd/emaildir/lists/ireval/msg00012.html

Louis Harris and Associates, "Judges' Opinions on Procedural Issues: A Survey of State and Federal Trial Judges Who Spend at Least Half Their Time on General Civil Cases," *Boston University Law Review*, Vol. 69, May 1989, pp. 731–762.

Malan, Douglas S., "Windfall Fees Come After Lengthy Battle," *Connecticut Law Tribune*, January 26, 2009.

Marcus, Richard, "Only Yesterday: Reflections on Rulemaking Responses to E-Discovery," *Fordham Law Review*, Vol. 73, No. 1, January 1, 2004, pp. 1–22. As of February 22, 2012:
http://ir.lawnet.fordham.edu/cgi/viewcontent.cgi?article=4005&context=flr

Marks-Beale, Abby, and Pam Mullan, *The Complete Idiot's Guide to Speed Reading*, New York: Alpha Books, 2008.

Maron, Melvin E., and John L. Kuhns, "On Relevance, Probabilistic Indexing and Information Retrieval," *Journal of the Association for Computing Machinery*, Vol. 7, No. 3, July 1960, pp. 216–244.

McKenna, Judith A., and Elizabeth C. Wiggins, "Empirical Research on Civil Discovery," *Boston College Law Review*, Vol. 39, No. 3, May 1, 1998, pp. 785–807.

Milberg LLP and Hausfeld LLP, *E-Discovery Today: The Fault Lies Not in Our Rules . . .*, 2010.

Mintz, Levin, Cohn, Ferris, Glovsky and Popeo, *2008 in Review: Developments in Electronic Discovery*, 2009. As of May 2, 2011:
http://www.mintz.com/newsletter/2009/Advisories/Litigation_0120_Adv_EDisc/KeyDev-inElectronicDiscovery.pdf

Mizzaro, Stefano, "How Many Relevances in Information Retrieval?" *Interacting with Computers*, Vol. 10, No. 3, 1998, pp. 303–320.

Morrison, Rees W., "Three Benchmark Metrics That All GCs Should Track," *Legal Times*, November 27, 2007.

National Association for Law Placement, "Class of 2010 Graduates Saddled with Falling Average Starting Salaries as Private Practice Jobs Erode," press release, July 7, 2011. As of September 23, 2011:
http://www.nalp.org/classof2010_salpressrel

O'Connell, Vanessa, "Lawyers Settle . . . for Temp Jobs," *Wall Street Journal*, June 15, 2011a, p. B1.

———, "New Work Rules for Temp Lawyers," *Wall Street Journal*, June 15, 2011b, p. B2.

———, "Objection! Lawsuit Slams Temp Lawyers," *Wall Street Journal*, August 3, 2011c, p. B4.

Oard, Douglas W., Jason R. Baron, Bruce Hedin, David D. Lewis, and Stephen Tomlinson, "Evaluation of Information Retrieval for E-Discovery," *Artificial Intelligence and Law*, Vol. 18, No. 4, 2010, pp. 347–386.

Oard, Douglas W., Bruce Hedin, Stephen Tomlinson, and Jason R. Baron, "Overview of the TREC 2008 Legal Track," *Proceedings of the 17th Text Retrieval Conference (TREC 2008)*, 2009. As of July 6, 2011:
http://trec.nist.gov/pubs/trec17/papers/LEGAL.OVERVIEW08.pdf

Orange Legal Technologies, "Electronic Discovery Pricing Estimator," undated. As of June 25, 2011:
http://orangelt.us/estimator/pricing1.html

Paul, George L., and Jason R. Baron, "Information Inflation: Can the Legal System Adapt?" *Richmond Journal of Law and Technology*, Vol. 13, Spring 2007, pp. 10–42.

Peck, Andrew, "Search, Forward: Time for Computer-Assisted Coding," *Law Technology News*, October 1, 2011.

Rampell, Catherine, "The Lawyer Surplus, State by State," *Economix*, June 27, 2011. As of September 8, 2011: http://economix.blogs.nytimes.com/2011/06/27/the-lawyer-surplus-state-by-state/

Recommind, "Law Firm Unearths FCPA-Relevant Documents Quickly and Cost-Effectively with Axcelerate On-Demand," undated. As of February 20, 2012:
http://www.recommind.com/sites/default/files/resources/Recommind_On-Demand_CSBrief_Anon.pdf

———, "WilmerHale Selects Recommind's Axcelerate eDiscovery," press release, February 1, 2010a. As of July 6, 2011:
http://www.recommind.com/releases/20100201/wilmerhale_selects_recommind_axcelerate_ediscovery

———, "Eimer Stahl Klevorn and Solberg LLP Selects Recommind's Axcelerate eDiscovery Platform for Next-Generation eDiscovery," press release, February 25, 2010b. As of July 6, 2011:
http://www.recommind.com/releases/20100302/eimer_stahl_selects_axcelerate_ediscovery

Roach, Michael, "Vendor Perspectives on This Year's E-Discovery Buzzword," *Law Technology News*, January 20, 2012.

Ronnie, comment on "Malpractice Suit Targets Quality of BigLaw's Temporary Lawyers," *ABA Journal*, August 5, 2011, 7:48 a.m. central standard time. As of September 22, 2011:
http://www.abajournal.com/mobile/comments/
malpractice_suit_alleges_negligence_by_mcdermotts_temporary_lawyers/

Roitblat, Herbert L., "Information Retrieval and eDiscovery," OrcaTec, 2006.

Roitblat, Herbert L., Anne Kershaw, and Patrick Oot, "Document Categorization in Legal Electronic Discovery: Computer Classification vs. Manual Review," *Journal of the American Society for Information Science and Technology*, Vol. 61, No. 1, 2010, pp. 70–80.

Roscoe Pound Institute, *Report of the 1999 Forum for State Court Judges*, 2001.

Ross, Mark, *Ethics of Legal Outsourcing*, Integreon, July 2011. As of September 19, 2011:
http://www.integreon.com/phpapp/wordpress/wp-content/uploads/2011/07/integreon_ethics_whitepaper.pdf

Ruckman, Andy, "Practical Tips to Help Control Costs and Mitigate Risks in Ediscovery," *Focus Extra*, 3rd quarter, 2008. As of March 23, 2011:
http://www.acc.com/chapters/wmacca/upload/WMCCAinsert.pdf

Schieneman, Karl, "Will Judges Think It Is Okay to Use Clustering and Suggestive Coding Tools?" *ESIBytes*, December 20, 2010. As of February 22, 2012:
http://www.esibytes.com/?p=1572

Schlunk, Herwig J., *Mamas Don't Let Your Babies Grow Up to Be . . . Lawyers*, Vanderbilt University Law School Law and Economics Working Paper 09-29, October 30, 2009.

Schofield, Lorna, and Amanda Ulrich, *Summary Memorandum of ABA Survey Narrative Responses*, April 26, 2010. As of February 22, 2012:
http://www.uscourts.gov/uscourts/RulesAndPolicies/rules/Duke%20Materials/Library/Summary%20
Memorandum%20of%20ABA%20Survey%20Narrative%20Responses.pdf

Schulman, Amy, and Sheila Birnbaum, *From Both Sides Now: Additional Perspectives on "Uncovering Discovery,"* c. 2010. As of February 22, 2012:
http://www.uscourts.gov/uscourts/RulesAndPolicies/rules/Duke%20Materials/Library/Amy%20
Schulman%20and%20Sheila%20Birnbaum,%20From%20Both%20Sides%20Now.pdf

Schwartz, Emma, "New Reality: Temps Must Join D.C. Bar," *Legal Times*, June 27, 2005.

Sedona Conference, Working Group 1, "The Sedona Conference Best Practices Commentary on the Use of Search and Information Retrieval," *Sedona Conference Journal*, Vol. 8, Fall 2007, pp. 189–223.

———, "The Sedona Conference Commentary on Legal Holds: The Trigger and the Process," *Sedona Conference Journal*, Vol. 11, Fall 2010, pp. 265–287.

———, *The Sedona Conference Working Group 1 Membership Survey on Preservation and Sanctions*, submission to the Discovery Subcommittee of the Advisory Committee on Civil Rules, Committee on Rules of Practice and Procedure of the Judicial Conference of the United States regarding the September 9, 2011, Mini-Conference on Preservation and Sanctions, September 1, 2011.

Seventh Circuit Electronic Discovery Pilot Program Committee, *Seventh Circuit Electronic Discovery Pilot Program: Report on Phase One—May 20, 2009–May 1, 2010*, c. 2010. As of March 4, 2011:
http://www.discoverypilot.com/sites/default/files/phase1report.pdf

———, *Seventh Circuit Electronic Discovery Pilot Program: Interim Report on Phase Two—May 2010–May 2011*, c. 2011. As of September 23, 2011:
http://www.discoverypilot.com/sites/default/files/Phase%20Two%20-%20Interim%20Report.pdf

Shah, Kamal, "Enterprise Search vs. E-Discovery Search: Same or Different?" *Information Management*, undated. As of August 15, 2011:
http://content.arma.org/IMM/FeaturesWebExclusives/featurewebexclusiveenterprisesearch.aspx

Shaikin, Bill, "Lawyers Giving Anaheim a Break in Angel Case," *Los Angeles Times*, May 25, 2005, p. D5.

Sharpe, Nicola F., "Corporate Cooperation Through Cost-Sharing," *Michigan Telecommunications and Technology Law Review*, Vol. 16, Fall 2009, pp. 109–149.

Shonka, David Charles, *Compliance with E-Discovery Demands in U.S. Non-Criminal Law Enforcement Investigations*, October 2010. As of March 4, 2011:
http://www.edrm.net/resources/edrm-white-paper-series/compliance-law-enforcement-investigations

Skamser, Charles, "The Costs of eDiscovery," *The eDiscovery Paradigm Shift*, September 10, 2008. As of March 4, 2011:
http://ediscoveryconsulting.blogspot.com/2008/09/cost-of-ediscovery.html

Smigel, Erwin O., "Interviewing a Legal Elite: The Wall Street Lawyer," *American Journal of Sociology*, Vol. 64, No. 2, September 1958, pp. 159–164.

Soder, Chuck, "'Predictive' Software Eases Lawyers' Burden in Document Searches," *Crain's Cleveland Business*, September 27, 2010.

Southern California Edison, "Southern California Edison Company's (U 338-E) Reply Brief," *Application of Southern California Edison Company (U 338-E) for Authority to, Among Other Things, Increase Its Authorized Revenues for Electric Service in 2009 and to Reflect That Increase in Rates*, August 8, 2008. As of March 3, 2011:
http://www3.sce.com/sscc/law/dis/dbattach1e.nsf/0/B056256881B039BE8825749F006EE6F6/$FILE/A.07-11-011+2009+GRC_SCE+Reply+Brief.pdf

Spann, William B. Jr., "President's Page: Reforms Proposed for the Discovery Process," *ABA Journal*, Vol. 64, February 1978, p. 157.

Stevens, Alan A., "Knowing Your Way Around the Rule 26(f) Conference," *ABA Mass Torts Litigation*, February 1, 2011. As of February 22, 2012:
http://www.winston.com/index.cfm?contentid=34&itemid=4369

Stock, Richard G., "Timekeeping Revisited," *ACLA Journal*, Vol. 19, No. 4, Winter 2009.

Stratify, *Total Cost of Review (TCR)*, 2008.

Temp Attorney, comment on "Malpractice Suit Targets Quality of BigLaw's Temporary Lawyers," *ABA Journal*, August 5, 2011, 7:55 a.m. central standard time. As of September 22, 2011:
http://www.abajournal.com/mobile/comments/malpractice_suit_alleges_negligence_by_mcdermotts_temporary_lawyers/

Tomaskovic-Devey, Donald, Jeffrey Leiter, and Shealy Thompson, "Organizational Survey Nonresponse," *Administrative Science Quarterly*, Vol. 39, No. 3, September 1994, pp. 439–457.

Tredennick, John, "Shedding Light on an E-Discovery Mystery: How Many Documents in a Gigabyte?" *E-Discovery Search Blog*, July 7, 2011. As of September 12, 2011:
http://www.catalystsecure.com/blog/2011/07/answering-an-e-discovery-mystery-how-many-documents-in-a-gigabyte/

Trenchard, Robert W., and Steven Berrent, "Hope for Reversing Commoditization of Document Review?" *New York Law Journal*, April 18, 2011.

Trubek, David M., Austin Sarat, William L. F. Felstiner, Herbert M. Kritzer, and Joel B. Grossman, "The Costs of Ordinary Litigation," *UCLA Law Review*, Vol. 31, October 1983, pp. 72–127.

U.S. Courts, "Materials Produced for Mini-Conference on Preservation and Sanctions, Judicial Conference Subcommittee on Discovery, September 9, 2011, Dallas, Texas," c. 2011. As of February 28, 2012:
http://www.uscourts.gov/RulesAndPolicies/FederalRulemaking/Overview/DallasMiniConfSept2011.aspx

Vail, John, Center for Constitutional Litigation, *Letter to the Honorable David G. Campbell*, submission to the Discovery Subcommittee of the Advisory Committee on Civil Rules, Committee on Rules of Practice and Procedure of the Judicial Conference of the United States regarding the September 9, 2011, Mini-Conference on Preservation and Sanctions, August 16, 2011.

Vecella, Frank, Thomas Fasone III, and Cathy Clark, "And You May Find Yourself in a Large Document Review," *ACC Docket*, May 2009, pp. 82–97.

Voorhees, Ellen M., "Variations in Relevance Judgments and the Measurement of Retrieval Effectiveness," *Information Processing and Management*, Vol. 36, No. 5, September 2000, pp. 697–716.

Wang, Jianqiang, and Dagobert Soergel, "A User Study of Relevance Judgments for E-Discovery," *Proceedings of the American Society for Information Science and Technology*, Vol. 47, No. 1, 2010, pp. 1–10.

Webber, William, "Re-Examining the Effectiveness of Manual Review," *SIGIR 2011 Information Retrieval for E-Discovery (SIRE) Workshop*, July 28, 2011. As of February 5, 2012:
http://www.umiacs.umd.edu/~oard/sire11/papers/webber.pdf

Wells, H. Thomas Jr., "Statement of H. Thomas Wells Jr., President, American Bar Association Re: Congressional Approval of Federal Rule of Evidence 502," American Bar Association, press release, September 9, 2008. As of January 5, 2011:
http://www.abanow.org/2008/09/statement-of-h-thomas-wells-jr-president-american-bar-association-re-congressional-approval-of-federal-rule-of-evidence-502/

West, Tony, assistant attorney general, Civil Division, U.S. Department of Justice, *Letter to the Honorable David G. Campbell*, submission to the Discovery Subcommittee of the Advisory Committee on Civil Rules, Committee on Rules of Practice and Procedure of the Judicial Conference of the United States regarding the September 9, 2011, Mini-Conference on Preservation and Sanctions, September 7, 2011.

Whittingham, Melissa, Edward H. Rippey, and Skye L. Perryman, "Predictive Coding: E-Discovery Game Changer?" *EDDE Journal*, Vol. 2, No. 4, c. 2011, pp. 11–15.

Willging, Thomas E., Donna Stienstra, and John Shapard, "An Empirical Study of Discovery and Disclosure Practice Under the 1993 Federal Rule Amendments," *Boston College Law Review*, Vol. 39, 1998, pp. 525–596.

Withers, Kenneth J., "Electronically Stored Information: The December 2006 Amendments to the Federal Rules of Civil Procedure," *Northwestern Journal of Technology and Intellectual Property*, Vol. 4, No. 2, Spring 2006, pp. 171–211. As of February 22, 2012:
http://www.law.northwestern.edu/journals/njtip/v4/n2/3/

"Writ Petition Filed Against 31 Foreign Law Firms and an LPO," *Bar and Bench*, March 22, 2010. As of January 19, 2011:
http://www.barandbench.com/index.php?title=Writ%20Petition%20filed%20against%2031%20foreign%20law%20firms%20and%20an%20LPO%20%E2%80%93%20Immigration%20law%20violations%20also%20alleged&page=brief&id=597&gn=0